STAGING A SCHOOL PLAY

STAGING A SCHOOL PLAY

PETER CHILVER

B T BATSFORD LTD

First published 1967

Made and printed in Great Britain by
William Clowes and Sons Ltd London and Beccles
for the publishers B T BATSFORD LTD
4 Fitzhardinge Street London W1

Contents

Illustration 1 drawn by Janice Goldsmith
Illustrations 2 to 32 by Ann Powers

Foreword

This book is an introduction to all the varied arts and techniques which go towards making a school drama production a genuine dramatic experience. It marks out the work of everyone who is connected with such a project, from the producer and the actor to the lighting director and the front-of-house manager. In each case it aims at providing a few basic ideas from which the reader may proceed to explore and experiment for himself. No work in the drama can achieve any kind of excellence if the worker tries to follow written instructions without experimenting for himself. Staging plays is like any other art. You can read the rules which other people have formulated from their own experience, and you probably need to know these rules before you can begin to experiment successfully with breaking them, but you must eventually break them. So this book maps out various ways of thinking about many different questions, such as training school actors, designing sets, choosing suitable plays, and creating new plays within the school, and all this is written down with the expectation that the reader will go off and use this material as a means of sparking off his own inspiration and that he will eventually reach conclusions far different from those contained in this book. It is this individuality of approach which is not only necessary for successful work in school drama, but which also gives it its unique flavour and excitement.

I *General Principles*

What is the educational value of a school play?

The staging of a school play involves an immense amount of time, effort and thought. For many of the pupils who take part, it becomes the major event, not only of that particular school year, but often of their entire school careers. And in many subtle ways it may influence the way they think and work for the rest of their lives, for working on a school drama production develops self-confidence, and hence character and personality; it develops taste and judgment and provides the experience of working with a large number of other people towards a common purpose.

There is a difference between a 'good production' and a 'good school production', and this difference is not necessarily one that can be seen by the audience. It is often assumed that the mere fact that a pupil appears in a school production is in itself a justification for the work he has had to

give at rehearsal and at all the various stages of preparation for the performance. This presumes that acting in a school play is necessarily an educational experience. In fact it is nothing of the kind. Many school plays are incompetently produced or badly managed, and are therefore of no educational value to anyone. But even if the production is a good one and reaches a high artistic standard, the full educational value of the project can still be missed. For a school play is essentially a 'project'—in the educational use of the word. It is something of which the pupils partake of their own free will, it has a definite end in view, and its end-product is taken before the public for their consideration, criticism and enjoyment. But an activity ceases to be a project if everything is laid on for the actors in much the same way as it is in the professional theatre, where quite often the bulk of the company are little more than pawns in the hands of the producer, and the actual production bears virtually nothing of their own individual or collective endeavour.

From the actor's point of view the work given to a school production should be much more varied and interesting than the work given to a professional production, for the simple reason that he takes a much fuller part in the proceedings when he is at school than he does in the profession itself. Very often those young people who go on from school drama to the theatre as a career find the work far less interesting and enjoyable than they had expected, precisely because their role as 'actor' in the profession is such a restricted one. On the other hand a professional production such as Miss Joan Littlewood's *Oh What a Lovely War* was probably much more of an educational experience for the actors who were involved in it than are most school productions, for there the cast was involved in the preparation of the script, the developing of ideas, the improvising of scenes and in doing research into background material. This could well be used as a model for some school productions.

Wherever possible a school production should involve the pupils working on their own initiative and accepting responsibility for the finished product. Where, for instance, the scenic designs are in the hands of an art master, then he should have a couple of apprentices who learn from him the various principles and techniques involved. And they should be entrusted with some of the incidental facets of the designer's work, such as programme and poster design.

The play's the thing

Producing a school play is in itself a form of improvisation. You discover the resources of your school and build upon them. But do not succumb to the disease of playing at being a 'professional company' that is so common among amateur dramatic societies. The object of a school drama production is to utilize all the available talent in an artistic enterprise, and the basis of this enterprise is the play itself. It is on the play that the greatest energy should be expended, not on the accessories. One frequently sees school productions in which far more time has been spent upon painting the actors' faces, or upon building elaborate sets and costumes, than upon the actual production itself. The result is an evening of dreary embarrassment. Dramatic productions exist for the sake of drama, not for the sake of playing games at making a school hall look like a West End theatre. If you have skilled carpenters in your school, and they can produce a magnificent set for you, then by all means get them to do so. But if your school lacks either the personnel or the facilities, then dispense with scenery altogether, and build your setting around the use of rostra and perhaps furniture also. You can do a magnificent production without scenery. Many good plays actually come across better to their audience when they are uncluttered by detailed settings. The same principle applies to costumes. If you have neither the money nor the facilities to buy, hire or make costumes, then do without. Improvise around such costumes as you can muster among your pupils and well-wishers. Probably the most valuable technical aid to a production is the lighting. A good set of lights, say ten spotlights and a couple of floods, is far more useful than elaborate scenery or a vast wardrobe of exotic costumes. But here again you can make do without, and will in fact have to do so if you lack either the money to hire the equipment or the services of an electrician to supervise its use. In the course of its history, the drama has survived without artificial lighting, and splendid productions have been staged in broad daylight. They still can be. The most important part of the whole operation of staging a play is the time spent by the actors working under their producer on the script itself. The rest is incidental. You can do your play in modern dress, in the middle of the school hall, in broad daylight, and you can still create exciting theatre if your production is skilful enough and your actors are properly trained and rehearsed.

What kind of discipline is needed?

It is obvious that there is little educational value in a production that is poorly 'disciplined'. Rehearsals that are chaotic, and performances that are a back-stage nightmare seriously undermine the educational function of the entire project. Occasionally, such productions are nevertheless successful, for a producer may have flair and his company may have zest, and the result is enchanting despite the pandemonium that has accompanied its preparation. As often as not, however, such productions look as chaotic as they in fact are. What is meant then by good discipline in a school production?

(i) The company respect each other. In particular they respect each other's need for a good atmosphere in which to work, which implies that there is quiet and relaxation. It may or may not be possible for the producer to work with some of his players while the rest of the company are making whoopee at the back of the hall, but it is impossible for the actors to achieve genuine concentration while this is going on.

(ii) The company accepts responsibility for the production as a whole. This may be interpreted as the traditional 'team spirit' or one may put it on a more artistic basis and say that every member of the company considers himself personally involved in everything that happens. He is therefore interested to watch even those rehearsals in which he is not as an actor taking part, for his comments may be of great value to the production.

(iii) The company works generously with one another. This sounds a rather extraordinary claim, but it is a valid one. All actors, even the most accomplished professionals, need to feel the generous co-operation of those they are working with. If a player behaves superciliously at rehearsals, or appears indifferent to the production, then the task of those who act with him is doubly difficult and no one can give of his best under such circumstances. Acting on a stage is a very difficult job, and the actor needs the goodwill of those he acts with. The lack of this goodwill is always especially apparent when things go wrong on stage and in front of the audience. The right sort of company spirit can only be attained if each member of the company feels that he is employed to his maximum capacity. For this reason a pupil who feels badly about not having a particular role and who therefore refuses to take any part at all, is probably doing the production a very real service. Actors are only human, and they need to feel that their role in a production is a significant one. This does not mean that everyone has to play the lead, but it does mean that the producer must consider his choice of play very carefully, with a view to ensuring that no one is left waiting in the wings for two hours unless he is happy to be waiting there.

(iv) The company must know exactly what they are doing, both as actors on stage and as actors coming to rehearsal. Where an actor is manifestly incapable of doing what is expected of him, such as when he is incapable of punctuality, then he is better dismissed. In this way the work is made more straightforward and satisfying for the rest of the company. Much depends here on the care with which rehearsal schedules are prepared, for nothing is more likely to encourage poor punctuality than the calling of actors to rehearsals where they are not needed until an hour after the rehearsal has started.

(v) The standards set by the producer must be ambitious. On every aspect of the production the pupils should feel that a standard of excellence is expected of them.

What makes a good actor?

If a schoolmaster is about to embark on his first production and he is as yet unsure as to the basic qualities of an actor, it is useful to remember that an actor moves as much as he speaks, and movement and speech are the raw materials with which he works. Very often pupils are cast in plays simply on the strength of how well they can read a set-piece. Under this system, the boy who is best at reading aloud, and at sight, always gets the biggest part. Usually this is a mistake as well as being educationally unsound and unfair. Many splendid school actors are not good readers, and if asked to read an extract from Shakespeare or Sheridan, or from Wesker or Brecht, will stumble hopelessly. If the master is working in a comprehensive school he will probably find that most of his finest talent comes from the lower academic levels, but their talent will remain untapped if they are cast purely on their skill at recitation. In fact, many professional actors are hopeless at reading aloud from an unfamiliar script. But an actor who can improvise an interesting scene out of the mere fragment of a given idea will usually prove most useful in an actual production. And he will be even more useful if he is also athletic. The more athletic he is the better, for the more athletic actor or actress will in most cases move more easily around the stage, will be able to wear different styles of costume with relative ease, and will in general present a more complete 'presence' on the stage. He will also be able to fulfil some of the incidental roles of the actor with confidence, such as falling, fighting, fencing and dancing. A producer who finds that his leading actor is a member of the Judo club will have relatively little difficulty when it comes to his climbing up a ladder, or leaping from a balcony, or dying with a sword through his stomach or a bullet aimed at his heart. One has only to watch the extraordinary athleticism of actors such as Olivier and Finney to see this principle in application. Actors need to be agile and alert.

What makes a good producer?

The two basic qualities can be stated simply —enthusiasm for the play he is working on, and enthusiasm for the company he is working with.

What makes a good production?

A good production is one that constantly surprises and stimulates the audience. The less that happens or appears to happen in a play, the harder it is to stage effectively. Plays in which the emphasis is entirely on the dialogue and where the movement and scope of the production revolve around the subtlety of the actor—Wilde for instance, and much of Shaw—are usually best left to the most accomplished professionals. A good school production should utilise an enormous cross-section of the pupils' talents. If it employs music, singing, dancing, fighting, fencing, acrobatics, changes of scene, costume, lighting, and even of acting style, so much the better. A good production is always in a certain sense spectacular, not necessarily because it gives a realistic portrayal of a train crash, but because it surprises the audience with its repertoire of production techniques. The audience should go away from a school production feeling that they have seen actors doing things that they could not do themselves, and that they have seen a production which they could not themselves have devised.

Basic needs

The only absolute essentials are a hall of some kind and enough chairs for your audience to sit on. After these, the two most useful facilities are: a set of lights and a set of blocks or rostra. With these you can create any kind of drama that you choose. Contrary to popular belief you do not need a proscenium stage—i.e. a stage which can be curtained off so as to be absolutely hidden from the audience. A stage can in fact be a great handicap to a production and this is for two reasons: it can inhibit the actors, especially young actors, or it may be lacking in some of the basic facilities of a good stage. As far as possible a teacher starting work on school drama should try to think away

from the stage itself and towards using the entire hall. Feel free to use as much space as you choose. Develop an awareness of space. Think in terms of flexible staging.

Production costs

The costs of a school play will vary not only with the attitude of each particular headmaster towards school drama, but also with the facilities of the school itself. A fairly ambitious school production might be budgeted along these lines:

	£
Hire of costumes	40
Hire of lighting	20
Materials for scenery	60
Royalties	15
Printing costs:	
programmes	20
handbills	10
tickets	10
Make-up	10
	185

This is not to suggest that school plays have to cost this amount, though at the same time it should be pointed out that some school plays cost twice this amount. Obviously a big school, with a great drama tradition, which can rely on selling 1,500 tickets at 4s. each can afford to budget on a much grander scale than a small school or a school which has not yet got a tradition of drama behind it. Some school plays make a profit, but this is in fact unusual and difficult to do. Most school plays run at a loss, for the simple reason that a school play, like a play done professionally in repertory, simply is not presented for enough performances to achieve a good financial return. Sometimes this loss is in fact met by the profits on interval refreshments. Obviously, you cut down on your costs wherever the attitude or the facilities of your school compel you to do so. Programmes and handbills do not have to be printed professionally. Excellent work can be done on the school duplicator. Costumes are not essential, nor is scenery. You have to improvise within the limits you are set.

How can money be raised?

There are the obvious ways—raffles, sales, fêtes. There are also activities from which the pupils can advance their own experience of drama, such as vaudeville shows, old time music halls and revues. These are marvellous money raisers and need very little in the way of scenery and costumes. The performing of music hall and revue is an excellent way of training and developing young actors. There is a vast amount of music hall material available. If you decide to do a revue, steer away from professional material, a lot of which has been published. Build up an original revue from the talents of your company and from the school in general. Use partly material improvised by the company and perfected for the performances, and partly material written by pupils and masters. If you are starting a drama society in your school, it might well prove more valuable to start off with a music hall or revue rather than with a play.

II *Flexible Staging*

What is meant by flexible staging?

Flexible staging can mean any of the following:

(i) Bringing the action off the stage and perhaps putting the audience on the stage and around the sides of the hall so that the centre of the hall is used as the acting area.

(ii) Using the stage as one acting area and a built-up platform in front of it as a second acting area.

(iii) Using rostra and stage blocks as sets for different acting areas and to create different levels on which to act, thus breaking away from the idea of one stage, one acting level.

(iv) Using any or all parts of the front of house for the actors' entrances, in addition to the wings at the side of the stage.

(v) Going from one acting area to another in order to allow the play to continue without interruption rather than stopping the play while scenery is changed. The commonest example of this is the simple device of playing a scene in front of the main curtain while the scenery is changed behind it, or playing one scene on the main stage and the next on the apron stage.

In short, flexible staging does not mean revolutionary ideas that no one has ever heard of before. It means an imaginative use of the facilities available so that the play may continue and maintain its flow without being interrupted for technical reasons. It also means using the stage and the hall in such a way that their limitations are not apparent to the audience. Illustrations *2, 3* and *4* give a few simple examples of flexible staging.

Why is flexible staging necessary?

Flexible staging is necessary because of the inadequacy of most school stages. They may be too high, or may lack width or depth, or may be too far from the back of the hall, or the acoustics of the hall may be bad. Sometimes, of course, there is no stage at all in the true sense, just a slightly raised platform. It is important for the producer to become sensitive to the characteristics of a good stage, because otherwise he will work on a bad stage without attempting to compensate for its defects. In many productions one sees vast numbers of people crowded on to a tiny stage, or actors trying to make effective entrances from the sides of the stage where there is not enough space, or using parts of the stage as acting areas when they are in fact not visible to a large section of the audience. The solution is to bring the acting out among the audience, break away from the limitations of the proscenium, and create as much space for yourself as you feel the play needs.

How can flexible staging be studied?

The secret of good staging is having a good sense of space. To give the simplest example, a king cannot make a majestic entrance across a distance of three yards, but he may be able to make a magnificent entrance across a distance of thirty. As in everything theatrical, contrast is essential. The contrast for instance between a confined space for an intimate domestic scene, and the sudden use of an entire hall for a crowd scene,

is basically dramatic. A feeling for the imaginative use of space can be developed by:

(i) Watching almost any kind of dramatic entertainment, especially ballet. Note the way in which good choreographers utilise all the stage and create an illusion of even greater width and depth than in fact there is.

(ii) Studying any illustrated history of the drama. Note the various kinds of staging employed in the various historical periods. Note from this the enormous variety of staging techniques which have been employed at various times. Notice that there is nothing new in the idea of flexible staging.

(iii) Studying the use of space in paintings, particularly in the painting of crowd scenes.

Overcoming the disadvantages of poor stages and poor halls

Many schools have halls and stages which are inadequate. The platform may be so low as to be virtually useless, there may be no curtain, no wing space, and no exit from the stage to a room at the side or at the back of it. The exits may be at the opposite end of the hall. The answer is not to attempt to use the stage at all, but to use the hall along the lines indicated in illustration *1* where the acting area is the main body of the hall and the audience are seated on three sides (including the stage), where rostra are used to create various acting levels, and the end of the hall opposite the stage is left free to allow the actors to make effective entrances and exits. Imaginatively used, this kind of staging can be immensely effective. The rostra are to be used

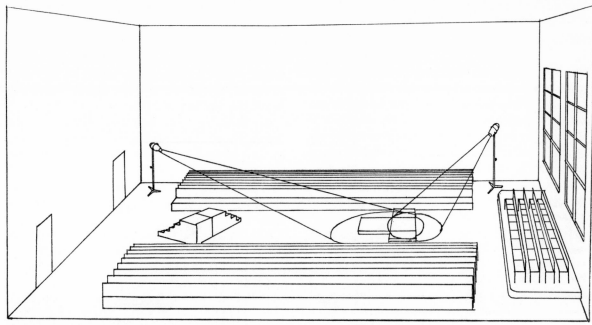

1   Adapting to the inadequacies of the hall

however the producer likes; they can be left there permanently or moved around in the action of the play, and they can be joined up or used separately.

Some halls have stages which are better than the one shown in the first two illustrations but they are nevertheless handicapped by various defects:

1   They are too shallow or too narrow.
2   There is insufficient wing space.
3   There is no wing space at all.
4   There is a sudden drop at the side of the stage to the floor level of the rest of the hall.
5   The stage is simply too small for the rest of the hall.
6   The stage is too high.
7   The stage is built without any thought for the acoustics of the hall.

How can these various defects be overcome? You can, of course, do the same as in illustration *1* and forget the stage altogether. But the stage, despite its defects, may have certain excellent amenities which you want to use; it may have excellent width for instance. The answer is to add a platform stage in front of the main stage, or if you cannot beg, borrow, purchase or steal enough rostra to make up a platform then simply place steps in front of the stage so that the actors can move up and down these to an acting area on floor level in front of the stage. With the addition of this apron stage or forestage you now have two acting areas at two different levels. (As a general policy the apron stage should never be on the same level as the main stage but slightly lower.) It is useful to remember that if you are using a

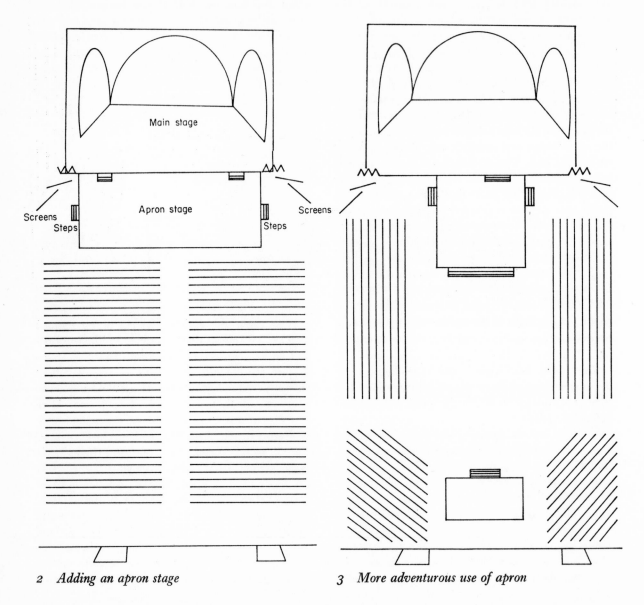

Main stage

Apron stage

Screens

Steps

Screens

Steps

2 *Adding an apron stage*

3 *More adventurous use of apron*

stage which is too high, as many school stages are, then you should use only the downstage area as your acting area (i.e. the area nearest to the audience). Avoid setting action right up stage, unless you are fortunate enough to have a stage which is below the level of the audience.

Illustrations *2* and *3* show a couple of contrasted ways of using an improvised platform stage in front of the main stage. The same quantity of rostra is used in both cases, but in illustration *3* they are split up into a smaller platform just below the main stage and another one at the opposite end of the hall. The audience are facing inwards to the centre of the hall. Notice that when you add different acting areas in addition to the main stage, you are not restricted necessarily to using one acting area for one setting and another for another setting. You can let the action spill over from one area to another as much as you like. If, for instance, you are using the main stage for all interior scenes and the apron for exteriors, there is no reason why the movement should not flow from the main to the apron stage even during one scene.

Using existing facilities to the full

Some schools have superb stages and superb halls. Whatever type of stage or hall you have, use every facility that it offers. Experiment until you are satisfied that there is nothing that you have neglected. Some stages today are built with small halls at the back of them, separated by sliding panels which in turn are covered with curtains or a cyclorama back-cloth. In that case use the curtains where it is convenient and the back-cloth too, and if there is an appropriate moment do not be afraid suddenly to open up the whole stage and add the hall at the back. Obviously you will not use this as an acting area but you may be able to use it for a grand entrance or for a sudden vista. If you have traverse curtains—i.e. curtains which can be pulled to cut off the back half of the stage—then these too may be of immense use at particular moments.

III *Choosing the Play*

The cast and the play

A good school production is usually decided upon with a particular cast in mind. In general, do not choose the very play you have always wanted to produce and then cast around for suitable players. Begin by discovering as much as you possibly can about your company. Get them to do plenty of improvisations. Observe the sort of characters they instinctively tend to choose for themselves when improvising. Listen carefully to the rhythms of their speech. Notice the kind of movement they have, and how they move when they are performing. And choose your play accordingly. Much will depend on the traditions and experience of the company, as well as upon the personalities of the individuals concerned. If you have a cast of Cockneys, possessed of great natural exuberance but lacking any kind of experience of working on stage, do not waste their talents on an attempt to do *Saint Joan* or *Macbeth*. If you have a cast of spirited Liverpudlians, find something where they can be spiritedly Liverpudlian. Do not be afraid of type-casting. If you have a cast which is not particularly academic avoid plays which demand great intellectual resourcefulness on the part of the actor—find plays whose meaning and significance is fairly straightforward. Where it is at all possible the play chosen should give scope to the school's musical talents as well as its dramatic talents. This does not mean you have to pick Gilbert and Sullivan, but try to find a play to which songs can be added even if they are not already there. Do not expect your leading actor to be a superb singer, and do not expect your best singer to be a superb actor, but encourage your actors to sing in a modest way, and your singers to stretch themselves sufficiently to do a little acting. Here again, an initial experience of music hall will help both you and your company to see their potential.

Unless it is absolutely impossible, always work with mixed casts. Some teachers apparently prefer to work with all-boy or all-girl casts, and will go into rapturous praise for Smith of the lower third who was so wonderful as Ophelia, or Susan of the sixth who was quite incredible as King Lear, but this is not only questionable as a dramatic device, it also discards the most educational facet of a school production—the chance for young people, boys and girls, to work together. If your school is a single-sex school, then set about establishing a liaison with a nearby girls' or boys' school, as the case may be. Failing this, contact local youth clubs and church clubs and see if you can draw suitable talent in this way from pupils of a wide variety of schools. The gain to your production will be incalculable, and so will the enjoyment and social value of working in it.

Which play?

Before you decide which play to do, you might consider first the different kinds of production upon which a school company can embark:

(i) *Revues, music hall and variety bills* Every drama club ought to produce something in this idiom every so often. They help to develop an extrovert style and to build up the confidence of the players without imposing the strain of carrying a large part through an entire performance.

(ii) *Established plays* A list of established plays which are suitable for school production would presumably be as long as the list of plays that have ever been presented by schools. The following is merely intended to offer suggestions for the kind of plays which have proved specially successful in school productions, which lend themselves to

very flexible staging, and which in most cases call upon the resources of a large cast:

Chips with Everything	Wesker
Left-Handed Liberty	Arden
Italian Straw Hat	Labiche
The Matchmaker	Wilder
Our Town	Wilder
Noah	Obey
Bartholomew Fair	Jonson
The Government Inspector	Gogol
The Lark	Anouilh
She Stoops to Conquer	Goldsmith
Under Milk Wood	Thomas
The Beggars' Opera	Gay
Oh What a Lovely War	Theatre Workshop

Adaptations of:

Treasure Island
Oliver Twist
Lord Arthur Saville's Crime

(iii) *New material* This may be of a *completely original* kind, or it may be adapted from other material, perhaps from a famous novel. In either case it may be written by a member of staff, a pupil or a local writer. Original material has the great advantage that it can be geared to the particular company that you are working with. Apart from the writing of completely original material, interesting work can be done with:

(a) *Adapting novels* The works of Dickens cry out for dramatisation, especially *David Copperfield*, *Oliver Twist* and *Great Expectations*. Very often professional adaptations of such works already exist, but have a look round and see if they are exactly what you want, and if not, see if there is somebody in the school who can do an adaptation specially for the school. Adaptations of works of writers who are either still alive or have died within the last fifty years can only be made with the permission of the author or his agents.

(b) *Documentaries* These are dramatic entertainments revolving around specific themes such as an historical event or character. *Oh What a Lovely War* is an example of this genre. This is a fascinating type of entertainment whose possibilities have not yet been fully explored. Until recent years such entertainments were confused with those rather dreary pageants where thousands of extras charged around the hall or the vicarage garden dressed up as Roman soldiers, while teacher or vicar spoke a rather lengthy commentary over the loudspeaker. There is in fact no reason why the 'newspaper' or 'revue' type of play should not be first-class drama. The range of topics you can pick is quite limitless —*The Story of Education, Blitz, The Great Fire* are typical examples of the kind of subject that offers great scope in terms of using existing material from many varied sources and adding to it the improvised material of the cast and perhaps pieces specially written by staff and pupils.

(c) *Improvised material* If your company are good improvisers, and have plenty of experience in this field, you can build up plays, or revues, or documentaries from their improvised material. You do not have to use material that is actually improvised at the performances themselves, though you can do so if you wish. The usual idea is that the company improvise and polish their improvisations at rehearsal until they are left eventually with a complete script.

Casting the play

A few general principles may be offered:

(i) Do not cast on the strength of readings; they can be very misleading. Not only are some good actors poor readers, but many good readers are atrocious actors.

(ii) Give the players various improvisations, either alone or in groups, in which they have to improvise the sort of character they might take in the play, in an analogous situation.

(iii) Avoid giving long parts to players who have not acted before. By all means give newcomers a fair slice of the cake, but they need to have had some experience before they can do justice to sizeable roles.

(iv) Do not expect a player to be able to change himself too completely for a role. If a boy does not have strong powerful movement, then do not ask him to play an aggressive and domineering character. All actors, even the most accomplished professionals, work within an area limited by the nature of their movement and personalities, or what you might call their psycho-physical characters. This does not mean that you cast on the strength of appearances, though this has something to do with it, but that you note carefully the range of roles which a player can reasonably be expected to cover. The fact that a boy is tall and hefty in physique does not necessarily mean that he can play a bully or a thug. His actual manner may be too lightweight and flexible, whereas a boy of very slight build may be ideal for such a role. Similarly do not expect an actor to change the entire rhythm and intonation of his speech unless you discover from his improvisations and his reading that he can do this without difficulty. Nor should you ask an unathletic boy to play an athletic role. You will merely submit him in that event to a long period of mental torture.

(v) Do not cast a player in a role in which he is bound to appear foolish in the eyes of the audience. If a girl is simply not beautiful, and is unable to acquire the air of being beautiful (which is probably more important) then do not ask her to play a role in which she is constantly referred to as a great beauty. Likewise, do not ask a boy with thin, knobbly legs to leap around the stage in tights if it is essential to the role that the character should look physically splendid. No amount of 'beautiful speech' can conceal physical idiosyncrasies.

(vi) Do not settle on your final cast-list until quite late in the proceedings. Make it quite clear from the outset that all casting is provisional and that you are going to try to give as many people as possible a chance to show what they can do. Perhaps use a double cast, in which the second cast act as understudies to the first. You must of course have every part properly understudied by the time it comes to the actual performances. The understudies should be given every chance to rehearse, and if they are better than their counterparts in the first cast then they should change places with them.

(vii) Try not to develop 'stars'. The temptation is sometimes irresistible if you feel that a particular player has phenomenal talent, but the process demoralises everybody else and hence harms the productions as well as taking the educational function out of the work. Do not give the same pupil leading roles in each successive year. Have a new lead each year.

How long does it take to produce a school play?

If you are rehearsing twice a week, for a couple of hours each time, then you should allow yourself about fifteen weeks or, say, a term and a half. Obviously the number of rehearsals will increase the nearer you get to the dates of performance. Avoid planning your rehearsal schedules too far ahead. It is usually best to plan only a month in advance.

Royalties

Royalties are payable for the performing of any play whose author is still alive, or who has died within the last fifty years. This applies to any kind of performance, and is not limited to performances for which tickets are sold to the public at large.

Choosing the play for the junior school

This book is written specifically with secondary schools and colleges in mind. A few general points may be made about play production in the junior school:

(i) Do not start thinking at all about public performance until your class has done a great deal of classroom drama and has become skilled at improvising. There are numerous techniques by which the teacher can develop the class to this degree of accomplishment. The simplest is to tell them very dramatic folk tales which they then act out in small groups. Do not ask all the pupils to show their work to the rest of the class, only those who choose to do so. Give them stories which have a firm dramatic line and where the characters pursue very clear-cut objectives. Very often young children like to keep on hearing the same story and to keep on improvising it, or to develop a repertoire of stories which they use again and again.

(ii) Keep the performance on the level of a romp. Do not drown the children in a mass of costumes and scenery and brilliant lighting. Do not play at 'grown-up theatre'. Preferably do not use scenery or artificial lighting at all. Do the piece in broad daylight in the middle of the hall with the audience sitting all around. Use the occasional rostrum to break the uniformity of the floor level if you think this is necessary. Do not fuss too much about costumes. Children can have their imagination sparked off by no more than a piece of material. They do not need to disappear behind a detailed costume in order to imagine that they are the king of the underworld. Often, all that is necessary is to put the costume box into the middle of the hall with various coloured materials in it, and the actors then go to the box and take out a piece of material and drape it round themselves as they need it.

(iii) Do not use scripted plays. Once the children are talented improvisers you can use this talent to create a play made up largely of their own ideas and dialogue. Take any theme which lends itself to episodic treatment, get them to do numerous improvisations around it, and carefully build up a play in this fashion. Take, for example, the story of the princess who could not laugh. Get the class to develop sequences of improvisations in which various characters employ varied devices to make the princess laugh. Let them dip into the whole mythology of children's favourite characters—Chaplin, the Wild West heroes, Robin Hood, the Ugly Sisters—whatever they choose. Add music, songs and dances. Throw in some sort of gymnastic display for good measure, perhaps having the gymnasts as part of the princess's wedding celebrations. Use the entire class, not just the good actors. Perhaps use the bulk of the class, either in groups or singly, to provide a commentary to the action. Develop the improvisations until they are well rehearsed and polished. Perhaps eventually ask the pupils to write the script down. This is one of many ways in which classroom drama can help to develop written as well as spoken English.

IV *The Production Team*

In some school productions one person takes on several roles at once. This is up to the producer to decide. But it is as well for everyone to have a clear idea from the start as to what his functions are.

The Producer is responsible for everything. It is his job not merely to direct the actors through the various stages of rehearsal but also to co-ordinate all the other activities that are part of the production. His enthusiasm and concern for detail provide the keynote of the whole project.

The Assistant Producer, apart from generally helping out the producer at rehearsals and making suggestions to him between one rehearsal and the next, also takes special rehearsal sessions with understudies and rehearsals where the producer is working with one group of actors while the assistant works with another. The job is an excellent apprenticeship for a pupil who wants to learn about production.

The Production Manager supervises arrangements for rehearsals, draws up rehearsal schedules, and acts as business manager, making arrangements as necessary for the printing of programmes and tickets, the hiring of costumes and furniture. He takes responsibility for publicising the production, securing free publicity wherever possible, through news items in the press or on radio or on television. Local newspapers are often keen to have short features or news stories connected with school plays, and the BBC will sometimes include brief references in area newscasts. This again is an interesting and valuable job for a pupil to undertake.

The Stage Manager is completely responsible for staging the play at the dress rehearsal and at the performances. The producer should not appear backstage at all at dress rehearsals or performances but should remain invisible somewhere in the front of the house. The stage manager follows the production from the very earliest rehearsals, noting down in his script all the producer's instructions to the actors, and ensuring that the hall is ready for each rehearsal and that any necessary props and furniture are provided and in place. The job provides a pupil with an experience not only of theatrecraft but also of working with other people and assuming responsibility for a complicated result. Quite often in school plays this job is taken over at the last minute by a member of staff. This is a pity, for not only are the results often indifferent, but also a genuine educational opportunity for the pupils themselves is therefore missed. In general, only one member of staff should be present backstage at a performance, and he should be no more than an unobtrusive presence who is there if he is needed. And if the production has been well managed he will not in fact be needed at all.

Assistant Stage Managers   The number needed depends upon the complexity of the production. Actors with fairly little to do in the actual play should be used wherever possible. But at least a couple of non-actors are essential. They are not usually introduced until the later stages of rehearsal.

The Lighting Director must have a sound knowledge of electricity so that he can work out exactly how to plug, wire and control the lights at the performances and so that he can cope with any emergencies, as well as being able to envisage the specific ways in which he will light the production. The producer and the lighting director usually work out a tentative lighting plan at the very earliest stages of rehearsal, for a good lighting plan offers the producer many opportunities which a poor one may deny him. The lighting director needs two or three assistants for the setting up of the lights and for the dress rehearsals and performances.

The Scenic Designer need not be a member of staff, but a pupil who works under a gifted art master on the design of sets and who learns much that may not normally come his way in the classroom.

Carpenters   Quite obviously the kind of scenery you can use is dependent on the resourcefulness as well as the facilities of the school's woodwork department. Generally speaking box sets are not only difficult to make but also less effective on stage than the simpler three-dimensional units (one of which may be very adequate for a production) or very straightforward stylised sets consisting perhaps of no more than a couple of rostra and a few pillars.

The Front-of-House Manager   He and his assistants are responsible for the sale of tickets prior to the performance, the sale of programmes and tickets at the performance, provision of interval refreshments, and for co-ordination with the stage management before the commencement of each act of the play.

The Costume Supervisor   Even where costumes are hired it is still essential to have someone responsible for alterations, cleaning and repairs and who remains backstage during each performance to handle any last-minute problems. When actors do not receive the actual costume they have to wear on stage until the very last stages of rehearsal then one member of the production team, perhaps one of the designer's assistants, should be responsible for providing each actor with a full colour drawing of the costumes he will be wearing. This should be done as early as possible. If the costumes involve long dresses or tights, then it is a good idea to insist from the start that the actors rehearse in plain rehearsal tights and the actresses in long 'practice' skirts. These can be bought quite inexpensively by the school and kept as part of the drama equipment. Practice skirts can often be improvised from various materials. In schools where all the costumes are designed and made in the school itself, the jobs of costume designer and of scenic designer are often fulfilled by the same person.

V *The Producer*

Getting ready

(i) Before the producer starts working with his actors he must study closely the limitations of his hall and his stage, including problems of acoustics and sight-lines. He must know how he is going to seat his audience, and how he is going to make use of such facilities as the stage offers him. He must decide whether or not he is going to add an apron stage and whether or not he is going to use realistic furniture or boxes and rostra or perhaps both. In other words he must visualise the overall character of his production, in terms of staging, designing and lighting.

(ii) He must become fully conversant with the entire content of the play, in both its general shape and in each particular detail. If it is a French farce then he must have a real theatrical knowledge of French farce in general and of this farce in particular. If the play is a period piece then he must know the period in its historical setting and be able to talk about the period to the cast, and also about the writer.

(iii) The producer should share this preparatory work with the cast. They, too, should be encouraged to do research into the period and the writer. Someone in the company, perhaps the assistant producer, should take charge of an enormous scrap-book into which any kind of clipping, or card or picture can be placed which has relevance to the play. All producers should keep a set of Trevelyan's *Illustrated Social History* by them, to use for reference and to show to the cast at suitable times. There are also many works on the history of costumes and at least one of these should be kept in every school drama department. Engage an artistic member of the company to sketch pictures of the various characters as he sees them and wearing appropriate costumes. All such work will illuminate the play for the producer and actors alike. If the school is anywhere near a good art gallery send the cast off for the afternoon to study pictures of the period depicted in the play, if this is at all possible. If a current film casts any light on some aspect of the play, then all the company should go to see it.

Moving the play

(i) *Working moves out in advance* Some writers urge you to come to your first rehearsal with all the characters' moves for the entire play worked out in advance. Bernard Shaw advised producers to take a set of chess pieces and use the pieces as models of the actors, and move the pieces around while marking on the script the various moves made. In this way you can see whether the moves synchronise or whether they are chaotic and confused. This may be an excellent idea theoretically, and some producers do indeed arrive at the first rehearsal with all the moves for the entire play completely worked out. The danger is that the moves simply won't work with your particular actors and that you will have to start again. It is certainly advisable to go to the first rehearsal with the moves worked out for the particular scene that you are going to deal with, and the scene should be a short one. But do not work out the remaining scenes in detail until you see how the company is progressing and how well you can anticipate the movement of the play without actually having the actors in front of you.

(ii) *The purpose of stage moves* A move on a stage must never be arbitrary or superfluous. It must be a definite move and must have a genuine dramatic purpose. Generally speaking there are two different reasons for giving an actor a move:

1   because he does literally need to go from point A to point B in order to do something, such as opening a door or taking a book from a shelf, and

2   because some psychological motive impels the character to move even though there is no material end in view. Thus a character may move across the room because he is suddenly disturbed by the thought of something or because he wishes to conceal his feelings. In such cases, we might say that his thoughts change direction and that the move is necessary to the character to express this change of direction. In all good plays this change of direction is very clear from the text. The move is part of the tempo and meaning of the scene, and without the move that particular section of the play fails to make complete sense dramatically.

(iii) *Fitting the actor and the move* Some actors, including some school actors, move themselves on the stage without more than a passing word from the producer. Some such actors move too much and generally flounce around the stage getting in everybody's way. But many are able to move with a remarkably good instinct and in fact give themselves excellent moves. It is a good thing to encourage actors, especially at the earliest rehearsals, to feel at liberty to move where they feel they need to. Quite often the actor spots the right psychological moment long before the producer does.

If an actor cannot cope with a move that you give him, do not keep on making him do it. Give him an alternative. If he would prefer to stay still, let him see if this works.

(iv) *The move must make sense* relative to everything else that is happening on stage and relative to the placing of the other actors, and of the sets and furniture. Do not give one actor a move that destroys what other actors are doing at the same time. One frequently sees productions where characters keep on moving across the stage in the middle of another character's speech merely to be in position for the delivery of their reply line. This can wreck the line of action of an entire scene. This does not mean that you must never move one actor while another actor is talking, but you must be quite sure whether the move or the dialogue is the more important at that particular moment, for the move will inevitably tend to absorb the audience's attention more than the words being spoken by the other actor.

Moves are sometimes wrong not because they occur at the wrong point, nor even because they take the actor *to* the wrong part of the stage, but because they are moving *from* the wrong place. As a simple example, it is difficult for a king to make a magnificent descent from a throne which is placed to one side of the stage and downstage. It is much more logical for him to come from up-stage centre. This is because the power of the character is less great from the audience's view-point when the move is across the stage than when it is downstage towards the audience. Very frequently the fault lies in the scenic design. How often one has seen a Lady Bracknell try to make a magnificent entrance through doors placed on the side of the set, and how much more sensible it would be to let her sweep in from upstage centre, preferably using double doors placed on a small platform so that her dominance is stressed by the dominance of her position and by the added height given to her by the platform at the very moment of her entrance.

(v) *Adapting the moves to the stage* The way in which you move actors must be influenced by the type of stage and type of hall in which you are working. If you are working in excellent con-ditions, where for instance the auditorium is raked so that the audience are looking down on to the stage, then you can use the full depth of your stage much more freely. But many stages are either too shallow or are too high up relative to the audience, and here the producer is compelled to work chiefly on the very edge of the stage just below the proscenium arch (i.e. the downstage). In this case it is essential to add an apron stage or simply to add steps down which the actors can come to create an additional acting area in front of the stage and at floor level. If you do use an apron stage, avoid using platforms which are the same height as the stage itself. Dramatically this is far less effective than having two or more completely different levels.

Similar considerations apply to stages which are too narrow. Do not attempt to put more on to a stage than it looks as though it should hold. Bring the bulk of the action off the stage and on to the apron or into the hall.

(vi) *The move must be right for that particular character in that particular play* This is a point which the scenic designer, as well as the producer, needs to keep in mind. Many effective-looking sets clutter the stage unduly and leave the actors too little room for movement. The opposite can also apply. If you are producing a play about a Victorian slum then the lack of living space should be a characteristic of the set and the move-ment of the characters should be restricted by a lack of space. If on the other hand, your setting is a palatial mansion or a Roman forum, then there must be plenty of space for your actors to move in. This is another reason for breaking away from the stage itself if it is inadequate. It frequently happens in classical drama, especially in Shakespeare, that a character has to run on to deliver a piece of urgent news. As often as not in school productions the messenger is expected to 'run' across a distance of three feet, pushing his way through a crowd. It would surely be more convincing to let him run literally all the way through the audience, and covering the entire length of the hall.

The rightness of a move for a particular character extends beyond the mere question of space for him to move in. If a character is highly indecisive, then do not give him forceful moves up and down the stage. The actor and the producer together need to think out how the character would move. Would he go directly to a particular point or would he tend to go round the furniture? Would he move quickly or slowly? Would he move often or infrequently? Is he the sort of character who would tend to place himself at a distance from others or would he tend to place himself firmly in their midst?

(vii) *Crowd scenes* When you are producing crowd scenes remember that you are manipulating five different things:

1 The actors themselves, including their costumes and their various appearances, and you can therefore mix and balance their grouping according, say, to the heights of your players and their costumes.

2 The set on which they are acting and the light that is falling on them, so that you can break up your crowd in different parts of the set and with different intensities of light.

3 The levels on which they are acting, so that you can have parts of the crowd at different heights from others.

4 The depth of the stage.

5 The width of the stage.

In arranging the actual grouping of a crowd all these five aspects should be borne in mind. Also there is nothing worse on a stage than a crowd that is lifeless, inert and unreal. A few pointers may be offered for the handling of crowds:

Use actors who are also playing other parts in the play, unless this is absolutely impossible.

Give them plenty of rehearsal time. Encourage plenty of improvisation at the rehearsals. In particular avoid the fatal trap of letting one character make all the responses while the rest of the crowd shout out vague grunts of agreement. Diversify the crowd's actions as much as possible. Get the actors interested in the behaviour of crowds. Get them to study the ways in which crowds do in fact behave at specific events. At the same time, make quite sure that the crowd know exactly what they have to do when it comes to the performance, for otherwise their improvised responses can drown the rest of the dialogue.

Pay particular care to the entrance and exit of a crowd. Do not ask a crowd of thirty to enter through a wing space that can only just accommodate three. Use the back and sides of the hall for such entrances. If the crowd has to 'rush' on, then let it rush through the entire length of the hall. Urge the players to use the space that the stage offers them. If a crowd is supposed to be a genuine crowd, drawn from a variety of places, then do not have them all entering from one direction. Similarly with an exit, do not ask a vast crowd of actors to leave the stage in a single second. If they are supposed to be drifting away from the scene of some excitement then let them drift, and do not encourage them to push each other off as if they were in a hurry to go. Fill the exit and the entrance with interesting detail, worked out very carefully in advance, so that the audience does not feel that the stage is being rather arbitrarily filled and then just as arbitrarily emptied.

(viii) *Contrast* As with all aspects of theatre-craft, contrast is essential if stage movement is to make impact on an audience. This means that an overall stillness is essential on stage, for otherwise no move achieves any particular significance and everything becomes confusion. The producer must look for these contrasts in the text itself and then transfer them to the stage. Contrast is essential to keep alive the audience's interest. Visual monotony, vocal monotony, and continuous movement are the most fatal ingredients, whether separately or collectively, to a dramatic production.

The producer at rehearsal

(i) *A word of warning* It is never a bad idea for the producer to deliver a cool word of warning, before the rehearsals get under way, that the school play is only a part of the school's many activities and only a part of the pupil's work at school. Rehearsing, learning lines, studying the play and the character—all this must be done without forcing other school-work into the background. Somehow the balance has to be maintained and it is as well for the producer to make this clear at the outset. The energy that goes into a school production should not detract from other work, nor should it antagonise the rest of the staff by turning the school into an improvised acting academy.

(ii) *Giving the actor his moves* Once the preliminaries are over, the producer's next job is to work through the play, scene by scene, giving the actors their moves. The actors mark out the moves on the stage and note down the moves in

pencil in their script at the appropriate points. Always ask the actors to write their moves in pencil and not in ink or with a ball-point pen, so that the move can be rubbed out easily if you subsequently make any alteration.

Up right (UR)	Up centre (UC)	Up left (UL)
Centre right (CR)	Centre (C)	Centre left (CL)
Down right (DR)	Down centre (DC)	Down left (DL)

- - - - - - - - - - - - Audience - - - - - - - - - - - -

4   *The acting areas of the stage*

Stage moves are given in two ways:

1 Reference to the areas of the stage (*4*). Thus an actor may be asked to move centre, or upstage right, or left of centre, and so on. Notice that Left and Right are always the left and right of the actor when facing the audience. In writing the move down the actor uses the usual abbreviations e.g. UL.

2 Reference to the furniture and scenery. Thus an actor may be asked to move to below the sofa, meaning he moves to the

side of the sofa nearest to the audience, or to above the sofa, meaning the side farthest away from the audience. Left and right of the sofa would again mean the left and right as seen by the actor when facing the audience.

Since the producer has to mark down in his script all the moves in the play for every single actor, he often finds it easier to give each move in each different scene a different number, and then to simply mark the number into the script at the point where the move occurs. He then inserts a blank page in between each double page of script on either side of which he writes the numbers of the moves for those two pages and the description of the moves.

The phases of rehearsal

Rehearsals usually go in four phases:

(i) Early rehearsals, where the actors are given their moves and are then given a few runs-through to allow them to get used to doing the moves. At this point the actors are working with the scripts in their hands and are making notes of any instructions that the producer gives them. It is often a good idea to give the moves of a scene or act (i.e. to 'move' it or 'plot' it) and then immediately afterwards to let the actors run through that scene before going on to the next one.

(ii) At the next phase of rehearsal the actors have attempted to learn their lines and are running through the play to familiarise themselves with the words and the moves, and are now working without the scripts in their hands.

(iii) In the third phase, the actors know their words and are running through the play to develop their performances and to allow the producer to stop them wherever and whenever he wants to, in order that he can get in detail the right performance at each moment of the play. In this way of working the producer does not interfere in the first two phases except to give moves.

(iv) In the last phase the actors give complete runs-through of the play without any interruption by the producer, but the producer makes notes throughout the run-through, and reads and discusses these notes with the cast immediately afterwards.

Whether this method works with school productions is up to the producer concerned. You may find that the actors simply do not understand enough about what they are doing to be left to their own resources in the early phases. They may need constant explanation as to what they are doing and the meaning of what they are saying. However much you may feel impelled to help an actor you must also give him time in which to develop his performance. You must not use all rehearsals for stopping the actors, though you must also, of course, use some for exactly this purpose.

Making yourself clear to the actor

Make your meaning clear to the actor in whatever way you can. If you can describe it in words, splendid. If you can do it by a combination of words and action, equally good. Some producers are very gifted at showing the actor what they want by giving an exaggerated performance of it.

This does not mean that the producer should end up with all his players imitating him, but he must be able to clarify what he is talking about and asking for.

Helping the actor

Actors are constantly meeting problems. The more inexperienced they are the more difficulty they may find in articulating their problems and hence the worse the problems become. Usually you can see that an actor is in difficulty simply by looking at him. How can the producer help?

(i) If it is a difficulty with a move, then you should again explain very carefully the reason for the move. Let the actor know very fully what he is doing. Sometimes the actor falls into difficulties simply because he does not feel any need to move at a particular moment and hence is in fact interpreting that moment of the scene differently from the producer. If it will help, show the exact nature of the move. Climb up on to the stage and demonstrate. Do not be afraid to point out what seems to you perfectly obvious. But do not expect an actor to do what you want the minute he realises what is needed. If you have been going over and over a particular point and then the penny suddenly drops it may be as well not to ask the actor to re-play that particular moment until the next rehearsal. If you simply cannot help an actor with a particular move, then the answer must be that the move is wrong for that particular actor or is wrong altogether. You must then either give him another move or leave him free to experiment.

(ii) The actor may have enormous difficulty with the delivery of a single line. He may feel quite unable to say it convincingly. This may be either because he cannot understand what the line means or because he cannot cope technically with the demands that the delivery of the line makes upon him. In the first instance you must talk about the line in as many ways as you like, until its meaning becomes clear to him. In the second case you must yourself show him how the line can be done technically. Suppose that an actor has to make an entrance in a crowded ballroom, and has to stroll around rather elegantly until his attention is riveted upon a beautiful lady who is dancing on the other side of the stage. In a film such moves are very simple because the camera establishes the line of dramatic development for both the actor and the audience alike. On stage the same thing can be very difficult because the audience's attention cannot be finally directed on anything, least of all when there is a crowd of moving actors on a stage. A young actor might well find such a sequence very difficult. He may perhaps find it impossible to mark off the first phase, where he simply strolls around with elegant ease, from the second, where he suddenly notices the beauty. He may find it difficult to really notice the one particular lady. In such cases the producer can rightly show the actor exactly what he wants. This will not only clarify to the actor what he is doing, but will also quite possibly show the producer various details that he has himself not properly attended to, such as the position of the actor and the other actors on the stage. It is also a good idea in such cases to break the action down for the actor into all its component parts. Instead of the actor thinking of it as one unit he should subdivide it into its details: he enters, advances to point of vantage where he can view all the ladies, carelessly looks around the room without expecting to see anyone of interest, his expectations are confirmed, he turns to go, he decides to take another look, notices an attractive face, takes a careful look, is most intrigued, moves towards her. The details of such a sequence simplify the job for the actor by enabling him to see clearly what he is doing.

(iii) Producers should be wary of creating unnecessary difficulties for an actor. This can easily happen if the producer makes criticisms of an actor which the producer is unable to put right. Do not say something is wrong unless you can solve it.

(iv) One way of handling the actor's difficulties is by giving him not just one alternative to the particular way of handling a line or move but several alternatives, and further to encourage the actor to produce additional alternatives of his own. Constantly encourage the actor's initiative. Welcome his ideas.

(v) Use improvisations wherever possible to help the actor out of his difficulty. If, for example, in the case already quoted, the actor cannot cope with the ballroom sequence convincingly, then let the whole company create various improvisations on this and related themes. From this it may be that the actor will suddenly find exactly the right interpretation of the scene and that the scene will become real to him.

(vi) Many actors get into difficulties because they try to *feel* what they are acting, instead of *doing* what they are supposed to be doing. The actor cannot see himself at the moment when he is acting and hence he often tends to rely on how he is feeling to tell him how well he is doing. The trouble is that feeling is something so elusive and vague as to be misleading. The actor should be encouraged to stop wondering about how he feels. If he is supposed to be feeling happy, as a particular character at a particular moment in a play, then he does not himself as an actor have to feel happy. All he must do is to perform the actions given to the actor by the writer and producer in exact detail, and from the point of view of the audience he will then be playing the character correctly. The question in acting is never how am I feeling but simply what am I doing? Actors should never bother about the creating of moods and feelings inside themselves.

Because of this obsession with mood and feeling, many actors find it much easier to play unhappy and depressed characters than they do to play happy and bright ones, simply because the energy that goes into feeling happy is so much greater than the energy that goes into feeling bored or demoralised. But the actor does not have to feel happy in order to play a happy character, any more than he needs to feel homicidal in order to play a murderer.

Another good reason for discouraging actors from bothering about their feelings is that feeling is a solitary and introspective occupation. One does not communicate by way of the feelings, nor do feelings create action. But acting on a stage is a series of actions, usually performed with at least one other person. In fact one of the commonest causes of difficulty among school actors is that they are trying to act on their own instead of with others; they are attempting to carry on as if nobody else on the stage existed. This is another way in which improvisations may be tremendously useful in creating the right basis for a performance, for they can suddenly open an actor's eyes to the reality of the other characters around him. For example in the case of the entrance to the ballroom, the real problem may be that the actor is so intent upon *showing* that he suddenly sees a great beauty that he does not in fact see any one at all, least of all a great beauty. In improvisation this can be ironed out by the simple device of making the actor spot a series of different people for quite different reasons and without knowing in advance who the particular people will be. Perhaps ask him to spot the person who is wearing a blue silk tie, or the tallest person in the room. Suddenly the reality of what he is doing, the fact of there actually being someone else whom he does actually see, will come home to him.

(vii) The other most common difficulty is that the actor tries to do too much. A frequent fault is to use the face as a kind of registry office of every thought and feeling that the actor thinks his character is experiencing. You must assure your actor that acting is less complex than that, and more true to life. The eyes do much more work than the face, which tends to do remarkably little unless there is some very special need for it. Never pull faces on a stage unless you would also do so in the same circumstance in real life. Facial stillness is essential to a good performance. It is the eyes that carry the thought and soul of a person, not the facial expressions.

Another way of doing too much is to use too many gestures. The producer can help in this matter by encouraging the actor to gesticulate as little as possible but to feel free to make a clear and pointed gesture whenever it is dramatically necessary. It is not helpful to an actor to say 'Don't gesticulate at all', for this can itself be tremendously difficult. If an actor feels a great need to move his arms and hands, then suggest to him a few very specific gestures that he can legitimately use. If he is playing a Dickensian lawyer, work out with the aid of prints of the period some appropriate gestures. Similarly if he is playing an Edwardian Duke, deduce from the costumes of the period and the very style of the play the kind of gestures that the character might well employ. It is good that an actor gesticulates if he does it confidently and knows exactly what the gesture is, and if he carries the gesture into his general movement so that it becomes a real part of the character.

(viii) Finally, if it will help an actor, and some definitely need such help, give him every direction down to the minutest detail. Show clearly how the line must be inflected and stressed if it is to make sense, show how the character moves, sits, talks, walks; show how the character sustains the thought of a line through the other characters' lines—give him everything he needs to see and understand what he is supposed to be doing. Not all actors need such concentrated attention but even very good ones may well do so. In their first experience of acting, and especially when they play leading roles for the first time, actors may need guidance all the way. They may have all the basic equipment for playing a role extremely well, but to achieve their potential they may need one hundred per cent assistance.

VI *The Actor*

The actor's dilemma

Bernard Shaw once wrote that the business of the actor is (a) to make the audience believe that real things are happening to real people, and (b) to be 'extraordinary'.

In other words he must be effective and exciting without becoming absurd and implausible. He must be real but also remarkable. In the balancing of these two qualities lies the great dilemma and the artistry of acting.

Learning about acting

Acting is not something that can be learnt from books. It can be learnt only from personal experience and from watching other actors at work. By reading about acting, as well as by watching it and talking about it, you can however help yourself to see the actor's problems more clearly. But this needs to be backed up by a lot of personal experience on stage. Be very careful of any 'theories' of acting, and be especially suspicious of any theory which professes to tell you the last word on the subject.

Acting with other actors

Acting is an action performed with the other actors who are on the stage with you. For this reason it is not possible to work on a part entirely on one's own. A lot of research and study can be carried out in private, but, especially with the inexperienced actor, the more work he does with other actors the better. Never act in isolation from the other actors on stage. There are some actors who are permanently unaware of the other actors around them and yet they very firmly believe that they act with them. A good way to discover what it in fact means to act with someone, as opposed to simply throwing lines at him in the expectation that he will come up with his lines on cue, is to watch other actors at work. Watch closely how far they convince you that they are truly listening to what the other person is saying, how far they direct their thoughts and intentions to the characters around them. The mere exercise of watching others will probably help you to do the same yourself.

Being effective

All actors need to be effective. You cannot give a good performance without being effective for then you are simply unnoticeable, and few parts are written by playwrights with a view to their being unnoticeable. But what does effective mean? It obviously means something quite different for every part ever written. A few general suggestions may be made:

(i) Acting is a very extroverted form of behaviour. It demands a certain kind of daring and wildness. There is something very daring about every good performance. There is something very daring about the mere fact of walking on to a stage and asking the audience to accept you as Banquo or Lady Windermere or whoever else you happen to be playing. It is important to note that the actor is in fact less daring at performances than he is at rehearsal. One of the functions of rehearsal is to allow the actor to experiment with his role and discover how far he can go, and what he can and cannot do. An actor who never dares to go over the top at rehearsal is unlikely to give a particularly good performance.

(ii) To be effective an actor must be able to stand on his own. The fact that acting is a team enterprise should not blind anyone to the fact that ultimately what he does must be done by him on his own.

(iii) Often an actor has to be able to make a very marked effect the moment he enters a stage. How does an actor make an effective entrance? Here again there is no single answer, but first he should watch other actors coping with the same problem. Obviously no two characters will make quite the same entrance, and the way in which the actor studies the question of his entrance depends upon his conception of his part and of the play and upon what he interprets as the character's intention at the moment of entering. A good entrance is, among other things, one which clearly tells the audience what the character is actually doing at that moment. Many entrances demand colossal nerve on the part of the actor—particularly the magnificent entrances of kings and queens. This kind of nerve can often be best cultivated by working in media such as the old time music hall, where the actor has to muster the confidence not only to come on to the stage but also to come face to face with his audience and entertain them.

Projection

Experience of music hall also tends to teach actors a great deal about projection. When we speak of an actor's projection we mean something more than his being heard. It is perfectly possible for an actor to be heard without his being understood. It often happens, especially in classical drama, that a lot of the text is difficult for both the actor and the audience to understand, and it may be difficult for the actor either to understand what he is saying or to project its meaning to the audience. To project means to convey to the audience the dramatic meaning of what is being said and done, and this includes of course those members of the audience who are sitting farthest away as well as those who are sitting in the front row. But it is not the same thing as shouting. To be able to project you must:

(i) understand the meaning of what you are saying in complete detail;

(ii) intend to convey that meaning to the audience. This means that you cannot project accidentally, and that you must concentrate all the time you are acting. This also means that even if your lips and tongue continued to deliver the lines through sheer habit, you would almost certainly fail to project the meaning of what you are saying unless you were also concentrating. This is one of many reasons why acting is hard and exhausting work;

(iii) be able to make your voice carry through all the parts of the hall where you are playing, but this does not mean that you should shout. Shouting is something which in real life one indulges in only at moments of unusual stress. Hence the audience will be most perturbed if you appear to be shouting in the middle of a quiet domestic scene. When the actor projects his voice he adds to the volume of sound he produces, without appearing to produce any vocal effort. In this sense projecting and shouting are quite opposite to one another. Vocal projection cannot be taught. Of all the attributes of an actor it is probably the most instinctive. A true actor will always be thinking of all the parts of the audience and of the projection of his performance. As a general rule, if you think of projecting to the farthest reaches of the hall then you will in fact project there. You have to direct your performance over the entire hall or theatre, and not only over certain parts of it. As an illustration of this one might quote the case

of professional actors of the not too distant past who used to be criticised for 'playing to the gallery'. This did not mean that they spent their entire performance looking up at the gallery, but that they were quite obviously directing their voice and their thought to the gallery, and that those in the other parts of the house did actually feel that they were somehow getting less of the performance than were their colleagues in the gods. This simply bears out that an actor has to direct his work at all of the audience all of the time, as well, of course, as doing many other things. The actor's concentration has to be strong and positive, able to ride over all kinds of distractions that the audience unwittingly creates, such as fidgeting, coughing, unwrapping sweets, blowing noses and appearing generally rather dissatisfied. Very often an actor has to address certain of his speeches directly to the audience. In some halls and theatres, the lighting accidentally lights up the front rows of the audience as well as the actors. In such cases the actor may be alarmed to see the look of infinite boredom that is written on the faces of the audience even in the middle of the most delightful comedy. In such cases the actor should not be in the least perturbed. Audiences almost always look bored and indifferent for the simple reason that as onlookers they are giving no thought to the expression on their faces;

(iv) be able to make the meaning of your actions clear to the audience even where they are unaccompanied by words. Actions must be simple if they are to be understood. Many actors try to do too much. Do not try to convey too much at one time. Many modern theories of acting unintentionally encourage the actor to clutter his acting with attempts to do a great number of things at one time. A stage performance is like life itself, you can only do one thing at one time. This is why, when you first look at good actors with a professional interest in their technique, you are struck by the extent to which they appear to do nothing. One of the simplest actions on stage, which many actors tend to complicate, is the action of listening. In life, we convey that we are listening to someone usually by looking at them. If we are very interested in what they are saying we also tend to stop moving while we are listening. Yet many thousands of actors attempt to convey the act of listening by doing strange things to their faces, such as assuming strange expressions, knitting the eyebrows, smiling or nodding the head in extravagant agreement. By performing this multiplicity of actions the actor confuses his audience, who see a chaos of moves on the actor's part, none of which they are able to interpret. And since the attention of the audience is probably supposed to be on the character who is speaking this is doubly disastrous.

A further point should be added to this discussion of projection. The audience will understand actions which you perform clearly, but it does not have extra-sensory perception. It does not know what you are actually thinking, or what you would like them to think you are thinking, unless this is revealed through some definite action or actions. This point is worth making because a lot of modern acting theory has encouraged actors to believe that they should stand on the stage thinking about their sub-conscious or the character's private fantasies. It is possible for instance that you are playing a character who you believe would spend half his time thinking of Battersea Power Station, and you may therefore waste a lot of time on stage trying hard to think about Battersea Power Station. Unfortunately

the audience will never get to know about this unless the fact is revealed clearly to them in word or action or both. What is going on in the actor's mind is irrelevant. The great thing is that he should concentrate on what he is actually doing.

One of the secrets of good projection, then, is that the actor does not try to do too much. The best performances are also the easiest to understand, the most clear-cut, and the most sweeping in their conception. You can play a part in many different ways, but you can only play it in one way at one time.

Timing

You will often hear it said that the art of comedy acting is the art of timing. This is true, but it may mislead you into thinking that timing is something that has to do with the delivery of funny lines and nothing else. It can also cause the actor to be rather afraid when it comes to comedy and to start worrying about his 'timing', a thing he may not do when he is in a straight play or tragedy. There are various points which should be made about timing:

(i) Timing is in fact listening. If you are really listening to what other people are saying and doing around you on the stage, then you will also have good timing. The actor who times badly is the actor who is not really listening but is simply waiting for his cue.

(ii) Timing is not limited to comedy acting, it is needed in whatever play you appear. It is most apparent in comedy simply because the comedic lines or the comedic situations draw the audience's attention to the tempo at which the actors are working. Comedy tends to make the audience think about the actor's technique more than serious drama does, perhaps because the mere fact of the audience laughing tends to disassociate them to some extent from the action of the play.

(iii) Timing is not isolated from the rest of the actor's technique. To time well one must understand exactly what one is saying and doing, and the timing of a specific line is effective only within the context of the rest of the scene. It is therefore difficult for an actor to time well in a bad production. It has been correctly said that a producer is like an orchestral conductor—he must blend the voices and movement of his actors to catch exactly the changes of speed and pitch which are necessary to make dramatic sense of the play. A good writer works with this orchestration constantly in mind. This is particularly so with Shaw, who had a highly developed musical sense and who also knew a great deal about the actor and his voice. In Shaw, if the lines are spoken correctly, and if the punctuation is scrupulously observed, this musical effect follows inevitably. The lines fail to make sense without it. With less skilful writers there is often no feeling whatsoever for the orchestration of the actors' voices, and the lines of the various characters follow each other with no more variety of pace or pitch than the lines of a company report. This is particularly so with most thrillers and vast numbers of so-called light comedies. There are however certain writers in whose dialogue the vocal variety may be very limited in terms of its actual range, but within that range remarkably subtle variations are needed on the part of the actor if the lines are to become truly dramatic. For instance, most French farce demands tremendous lightness and quickness and directness on the part of the actors, and they must be able to sustain these qualities throughout the play. But at the same time they must find tremendous variety within these limitations, so that the lightness constantly tends towards greater weight, the quickness tends towards a more sustained tempo, and the directness towards a greater flexibility. The skill of the actors in plays such as these lies not in going from one quality to another quality that is diametrically different but in playing slight variations on single themes. For examples of this you have only to look at the opening page of dialogue in *An Italian Straw Hat*, which demands tremendous quickness and lightness from the actors but which needs to be carefully phrased and modulated if it is to be meaningful to the audience.

(iv) Good timing can only be achieved in collaboration with the other actors on stage with you. A clumsy actor can wreck the timing of his fellow actors. The Gwendolen and Cecily scene in *The Importance of Being Earnest*, to quote an obvious example, cannot succeed if either actress is unsympathetic to the work of the other. The two play off each other both as actual characters in the play and also as actors working on their roles. Here again the point must be stressed that timing is an orchestrated effect in which the actor works with his other actors. If you are interested to read examples of scenes in which the timing of each actor adds up to an orchestrated timing of the entire scene you should read the scene with Bohun the barrister in Shaw's *You Never Can Tell* or the scene in Act Two of Pinero's *Dandy Dick* where the two army officers attempt to entertain the Dean's family with a musical evening. In each case the timing of each character perfectly balances the timing of the other characters and each one has to be perfect before the drama can be really effective. For examples of beautifully balanced timing in dialogue between two characters only, one might look at the scenes between Archer and Mrs Sullen and between Archer and Cherry in Farquhar's *The Beaux' Stratagem*.

(v) Good timing means a subtle feeling for vocal change, whether of pitch or tempo or volume. It is the sudden slowing down which is dramatic, or the sudden speeding up. Similarly it can be dramatic when a character suddenly sustains a thought with remarkable carefulness when that character usually reaches decisions with great speed. It needs tremendous nerve on stage to time correctly, and the actor needs to experiment very freely at rehearsal. In comedy the funniest effects are sometimes obtained through the delayed delivery or delayed response of the character. A classic case of this occurs in the opening scenes of the comedy *The Happiest Days of your Life*, in which a rather dry and sarcastic school-teacher produces an enormous scarf which his doting aunts have insisted on knitting for him. Handled quickly the sequence is quite unfunny, but if the actor dares to take his time in surveying the enormous length of scarf and slowly lets the feeling of disdain take utter possession of him, the effect can be delightful.

Here again, simplicity is essential. An actor who is trying to be funny in all directions as it were, is never funny at all. Likewise the variety of pitch and tempo is only effective if presented against a more or less stable background. A character must have a recognisable pitch and rhythm before the actor can start varying it. Much can be achieved through simply dropping the pitch unexpectedly, especially with characters who are being deliberately witty or sarcastic. American actors and actresses, and particularly American comedians, tend to be brilliant at this kind of 'throwaway' technique, in which the funniest lines are tossed away with seeming casualness under the breath.

(vi) Some writers maintain that a producer must never give an actor his timing. This is questionable. Quite often the producer gives an actor his timing simply by making the meaning of a particular line clear to him. Or the producer may point out that it is necessary for an actor to pause to think before he delivers a particular line. The producer has to orchestrate and co-ordinate all his actors' performances, and in this way he controls the timing of them all. The producer must in particular correct actors whose timing is wrecking the work of other actors.

Reading about acting

The most valuable writer on the art of acting is undoubtedly Bernard Shaw, who not only wrote well, but also knew an immense amount about the actor's craft and particularly about the use of the voice. Try to get hold of a recent collection of his essays and letters entitled *Shaw on Theatre*.

The actor's personality

Do not leave yourself behind when you go on to a stage. Exploit and explore your own personality and use as much of yourself as you can in each role you play. Some of the most exciting professional performances are those in which the actor adapts all of himself to his role. The dullest are those in which he disappears behind the character and the make-up.

VII *The Actor's Movement*

Various suggestions may be made about the way in which an actor should move on stage:

Stillness

The most difficult thing to achieve on stage is stillness, but stillness is essential in any performance. Without a more or less still background no amount of movement is effective. An actor who cannot be still is nothing better than a nuisance, and he should be packed off the stage at the earliest opportunity. By stillness is meant not simply stillness of the limbs but stillness of the entire physical apparatus, including the muscles of the cheeks, the eyebrows and the hands. You should pay particular attention, the next time you are watching professionals at work, to the extent to which they move their hands. You will find that actors use their hands remarkably little and that when they do use them they are doubly effective for that reason.

Posture

In real life a lot of us have appalling posture. We stoop and sag and generally behave as if we were crippled and diseased. On the stage, sloppy posture distracts the audience and makes it harder for the player to project the meaning of what he is saying and doing. An actor must be able to stand up straight and relaxed, and to move easily and comfortably in such a way that the audience does not lose concentration half way through while it stops to marvel at the actor's curious little walk or strangely rounded shoulders, unless indeed the play and the character both demand this. The same thing applies to the simple action of sitting down. The actor must be able to sit down without it seeming that he is on the verge of physical collapse, and without his appearing to perform *Knees up Mother Brown* at the actual moment of sitting. In real life, a large number of us do literally appear to collapse as soon as we feel the chair safely beneath and behind us, but such an action on the stage would disrupt the action of the play, unless again there were valid dramatic reasons for it.

But what is good posture on the stage? Very simply it is the way of standing, sitting or moving, in which the shoulders, arms and hands are relaxed and the back is held straight without forcing the chest out in the manner of a military parade. Military stance is the opposite of good stage posture and also the opposite of healthy posture. This is not to say that good posture on stage is effortless. If you put no effort whatsoever into your posture you will quite obviously collapse into a neat pile on the floor, but good posture appears effortless to the audience. In this respect again it is unlike military posture which even to the most indifferent onlooker is obviously brimming over with effort and strain. The effort in good posture goes chiefly into holding the spine straight. Many people do this without thinking about it, especially people who are of average height or are short. But tall people, especially when they are young, may be over-sensitive about their height and may try to reduce their height by walking with a bent back and rounded shoulders, and when they are standing still they may tend to bend their back and to stand on one leg with it slightly bent. The shorter person seldom gets involved with this kind of nonsense and he will, without thinking about it, tend to stretch his height to the utmost by straightening his back and legs. Tall actors may need to be reminded that if they stand up straight they will make everybody else look rather small. But if they stand up crooked they will make themselves look abnormal.

A further point about good posture is that the jaw should not jut outwards but should be tucked slightly in towards the chin, so that the top of the head is the highest point of the body. One of the characteristics of very bad posture is that the forehead tends to be pushed upwards and to become the highest point.

When you are standing still on a stage beware of standing with your feet together or even only slightly apart. This suggests to the audience either nervousness or diffidence. Likewise it is an obvious mistake to allow the toes to point inwards as this suggests a farcical degree of timidity. The feet should be placed a reasonable distance apart with the toes pointing outwards, and the whole posture should be sufficiently firm for the actor to be able to move from the static position into a walk without any shuffling around to find a new equilibrium.

Simplicity of movement

Many moves which in real life are instinctive and uncontemplated can present great difficulty to an actor on stage. This can especially happen with very minor moves, such as getting up from the sofa to get an apple from the sideboard and then coming back again. The actor may simply lose the character altogether in such a move, and may revert unconsciously to a style of movement which is peculiar to the actor and quite wrong for the character. Every move must be in character. Where an actor finds difficulties such as this it may well be because he is trying to hurry the move. Never be in a hurry unless there is a clear reason for it. Many performances fail because the actor is in such a rush. A move may also fail to work because the actor loses the relaxed but firm posture which he has been using while sitting or standing still. There is no necessity to start swinging the shoulders about, or to break into a little skip, simply because you move from one side of the stage to another. The back should, generally speaking, remain straight, and the shoulders, arms and hands relaxed. At first it may seem artificial to do this consciously, but it will in time contribute to the overall simplicity and clarity of a performance.

Sitting down

It may be objected that when an actor sits down, then all he is doing is sitting down, and there is nothing further to be said about it. But usually the actual motion of sitting down is incidental to something else, such as what is being said at that moment, and for this reason any clumsiness in the sitting down can be distracting and wrong. Also, of course, the actor may have a personal way of sitting down which is quite unsuited to the play or the character. Practise how to sit down without losing equilibrium and without appearing unnaturally stiff. Practise the reverse—rising from a chair without appearing to spend five minutes gathering oneself together. In life we often grab hold of chairs before sitting in them as if we were afraid of them running away before we have firmly ensconced ourselves in them. Avoid this on stage; it looks remarkably funny.

Stage falls and fights

The best way to prepare for stage falls and fights is to take a course of lessons in Judo, for this teaches you to make remarkably realistic falls without hurting yourself. The secret is consciously to take the weight of the fall on to a specific part of the body such as the hands. Suppose for instance that an actor wants to make a dead faint in which the body starts from a vertical position and falls through all the angles of a right angle before reaching the floor. The actor keeps his body straight, and then as he is reaching the floor he hits the floor hard with the palm of the hand that is not visible to the audience and the force of the blow takes the weight away from the rest of the fall. The great thing is to be confident about what you are doing. The same applies to fighting and fencing. If you are tensed up when you fall then you will quite probably hurt yourself. Practise repeatedly until you know exactly what you are doing.

If you have no experience of Judo, then the simplest preliminary style of falling is one that is often used in P.E. lessons in schools. In slow motion, the fall goes like this: stand upright and relaxed; relax the knees and let the bodily weight drop downwards but not forwards or backwards, so that you end up sitting on your haunches; then let the weight go forward on to the knees so that the knees drop forward on to the ground; now drop the weight sideways taking the weight of the drop with the hand on that side, and as you do so, swivel round so that the part of the body touching the ground changes from the knees and hand to the seat and hand; now let the entire body collapse and stretch out. Repeat this exercise until you can do it easily and unselfconsciously and each part of the move flows easily into the next. This is a very simple but effective way of falling, and once you can do it confidently you will be able to vary it at will. Any P.E. teacher will give you exercises to develop your skill in falling.

Stage fights are no harder than stage falls

except that since more than one person is involved it is essential that everyone should know what he is doing and be able to repeat the same thing each time. Accidents need occur in stage fights only if someone decides to add to or subtract from what he has been doing at rehearsal. They should be quick and simple and as stylised as possible. The actors should think of the fight in terms of phases. In many real fights, such as you may see in the street or even in a professional boxing ring, an enormous amount of the fight looks like nothing more than a general mess, in which a given number of heads disappear into an overall confusion. This kind of fight does not look interesting on stage for the simple reason that the audience cannot see what is going on. The general rule with stage fights is that a good deal of time should be spent with the participants about to strike each other, but not yet doing so. The preparation is itself highly dramatic. Shape can be given to a stage fight along the following lines:

(i) Preparation and build-up and a few tentative attempts at coming together.

(ii) A few moments in which the actors box one another. The force of a blow should be non-existent by the time it lands, and for this reason you should usually aim at the shoulder that is upstage and therefore out of the audience's line of vision. Never aim at the face.

(iii) A brief clinch or a brief wrestling session.

(iv) A break followed by some kind of dénouement. The simplest and the most effective to stage is to have one actor take a running leap at another, bringing him to the ground and landing on top of him. The technique is very simple. The actor who runs at the other does not in fact attempt to bring him to the ground, nor does he jump directly at him. If both actors are facing each other and are in profile to the audience, then in slow motion the sequence would go rather like this: the first player runs towards the second who is standing still, perhaps collecting himself together as it were; the first player comes to the downstage side of the second player so that he momentarily blocks him from the audience's view; he puts a hand on each of the other's shoulders and uses this to lever himself off the ground, kicking his legs straight out in front of him in order to exaggerate the force of the move; as he lands he breaks the force of the fall with his feet by striking the ground; he must be sure to land straight in front of himself and not to one side or else he will fall into the second player's path. At the same time the second player falls backwards, as if pushed back by the force of the first player and the second player breaks his fall with his hands. He also must be sure to fall straight back and not sideways. Since the first player will recover equilibrium before the second one does, he can in that brief moment climb on to the second and pin him down. It is important to remember not to jump square on to another character. In the manner suggested here, which is just a possible way of directing a fight between two characters, an appearance of leaping on to someone is created without it actually being done.

Where the players need to have a sword fight, it is essential that they should have a series of lessons with a proper fencing instructor. Two actors who enjoy sword-fighting, and who have had proper lessons will come to no harm on stage provided they agree to keep strictly to what they have practised at rehearsals. Here again, remember that the most important part of a sword fight is the preliminaries. Much use can be made of characters leaping from boxes or chairs and tables.

Unconscious movement

Stage movement does not mean simply the movement of the body from one part of the stage to another, but any kind of muscular effort, however slight it may appear. Thus when a character unconsciously straightens the crease of his trousers, or suddenly bites his finger nails, this is a movement. A character's every move, no matter how insignificant, must be under the actor's control and must be a conscious part of the actor's characterisation. For this reason it is again essential for an actor to be able to maintain complete stillness on a stage, for otherwise the actor's own fidgetiness will spill over into the character he is playing. It is useful to remember that a person's movement may be divided into two main headings: conscious movement, designed with a clear purpose, and movement made with no apparent purpose and often performed quite unconsciously, such as pushing one's hair back even when it appears to be perfectly in place, or coughing nervously, or running lightly over a table-top with one's fingers and for no apparent reason. The latter are often referred to as shadow moves. Every character will have his own distinctive way of moving, including his own shadow moves. A very academic person will move quite differently from a highly sensual person. The variations are infinite. Be very careful in your selection of shadow moves. Make an exhaustive study of the shadow moves of the people around you. Notice the superfluousness of much of the movement that they perform, its lack of economy, and notice particularly the movement of the hands. A study of movement for stage purposes begins with a thorough observation of other people. Note the different qualities of their movement, and see how far you can relate the quality of their movement to the quality of their characters. Having done this, remember that on stage, movement must be kept to a minimum if it is to be effective, and that no movement, however effective it is, should be allowed to clutter a performance.

Improving an actor's movement

(i) Watch other actors and watch the movement of dancers. Watch foreign films.

(ii) Watch other people, anywhere and everywhere. Look out for markedly different styles of movement. Note the way a boxer moves in a ring, a teacher moves in a class-room, a girl moves in a dance hall, or a preacher moves in a church.

(iii) Try to trace the connection between people's voices and their movement. See how far physical tension produces vocal tension, and how far physical ease and fluidity goes with a relaxed and relaxing voice.

(iv) If you hear of anyone in your locality giving classes in the Laban Theory of Movement, go along for a few classes and see if it interests you. Laban was one of the first people to make a study of the different ways in which different people move. He then attempted to classify these movements, and in this way developed his own vocabulary for analysing and discussing movement. To those coming new to it, Laban's theory often appears pompous and tortuous, but to the persistent it offers something of great interest. For the actor, it provides a clear basis on which to think of the movement of the character he is playing; for the teacher, it encourages a perceptive eye for physical tension and hence encourages you to think in terms of releasing tension rather than suppressing it still further. Laban has also exercised much influence in recent years on the teaching of P.E. in schools. The best way to study Laban is to go along to a Laban studio and become familiar first with the practical exercises that he developed, and then perhaps take a look at the theory behind the exercises. Unfortunately, Laban's writings are not very readable and in fact much of the theory has been developed since his death by his various followers. Very briefly, what Laban attempted to do was this:

(a) In his exercises, to devise ways of expanding the range of a person's movement. He worked on the supposition that our movement not only defines our personality but also limits it, and that therefore the wider the range of movement that we can master, the more we shall develop as people.

(b) In his theory, to describe and catalogue the various kinds of movement that people perform.

(v) Almost any kind of sport will help to give you a greater degree of physical confidence, provided you enjoy the sport in question. Swimming is the ideal sport in that it strengthens and relaxes the entire body.

General principles

(i) Every character moves in his own unique way, and his movement expresses and defines his character every bit as much as the words he speaks.

(ii) Do not move unnecessarily. Do not fidget. Stillness is the most useful quality an actor can possess.

(iii) Do not move quickly unless you definitely need to. Always take your time.

49

VIII *Rehearsals: Early Stages*

First rehearsals

(i) *The read-through* After the producer has introduced the play it is customary for the cast to sit down and read the play through. Whether it is worth doing this is often very questionable. Quite often the read-through is so dull and dreary that it proves a most discouraging experience for all concerned. As often as not it is a good idea to plunge straight away into moving the play.

(ii) *Giving the actors their moves* Depending on the complexity of the play, the task of giving the actors their moves can take a very long time. Make sure that the actors mark their moves down in the scripts with great care and encourage a precision of movement. There is often some member of the cast who thinks that everybody must rehearse his moves except himself. When it comes to the performance such an actor will either panic entirely or will move around the stage at random in what he believes to be a most dramatic and impressive fashion. This may be great fun for the actor concerned but it is torture for those who have to act with him. It also destroys all the work that has been done at rehearsal, for the actor's moves are the basis of the production. Actors such as this should only be tolerated when the producer asks all his company to do whatever comes into their heads. The production then becomes a kind of joyous battle in which anything goes and the play completely disappears. This is not to say that an actor must never be allowed to vary a move. He should be free at all stages of rehearsal to suggest that he try something differently from last time until everyone feels that the right move has been found. Then it should be consolidated. To say that you should carry on experimenting until the production is over and done with is the same as saying that anything will do and one way is as good as any other.

(iii) *Letting the actors develop* Give the actors time to develop their interpretations. This aspect of a producer's work is very difficult, for he must be able to distinguish between a totally wrong conception of a line or role, and a tentative groping in the right direction, and also between an actor who simply cannot give a performance of the kind the producer would like, and an actor who can do it but needs constant encouragement and guidance.

The actor at rehearsal and outside rehearsal

Rehearsals make tremendous demands on an actor's energy and concentration, every bit as much as do the performances themselves. It is always worth stressing, however, that rehearsals are not fully effective unless the company are working at their parts outside rehearsal time. There are some school actors who regard rehearsals as the place for doing everything that has to be done on their roles. Ideally there should always be a marked development and progress in the production, *between* one rehearsal and the next, and not simply *at* rehearsals. This means that a lot of work is being done privately by the actors themselves. Actors must be urged to practise what they are doing and to polish and perfect their work either on their own or, better still, working with other members of the cast. They should not leave everything till the rehearsal. This includes the learning of lines. As soon as an actor has his moves for a particular scene he should be prepared within a matter of days to go through the scene with the lines and moves learned. There are some actors who are able to do wonderful rehearsal work with the script still in their hands, but they are in a minority and are

seldom the inexperienced ones. Also, of course, they discourage everybody else from bothering to learn their lines.

What else must the actor do outside the actual rehearsals? In whatever way he thinks right for himself, he must study his role. This will mean that he will first read the play through carefully many times to see his own role in perspective, to see in his mind's eye what the character looks like, sounds like and how he moves. He will then re-read his own scenes with particular regard to what the other characters are saying and not merely to what he himself says. From these readings he will be able to construct the background of the character, and see why and how the character acts and reacts in the various situations in the play. From this he will then go on to discover all he can about the background of the particular play, its historical setting, its style, its costumes and social customs.

It is always worth stressing that not all actors work in this way, nor do they have to work in any specific way. The results are what counts. Some actors really do not know how they work and yet are splendid on the stage. Some actors give wonderful performances without exploring the background of either the play or the period or the character. Some instinct is at work in them and they feel their way towards the right performance in their own particular way. In this case, do not force an actor to be coherent about his methods if he does not want to be or simply cannot be. One often sees producers creating great difficulties for actors by adhering to some method of producing which forces actors to think and work in one way only. If an actor performs well at rehearsal, and is giving the performance you want, do not make him go into a long philosophical discussion of what he is doing. Only do this if he cannot cope with his role and if you feel that a philosophical discussion will help him to see what is wanted.

The actor uses his rehearsal time not only to develop his role in harmony with the production, but also to experiment with his performance, to see how far he can go with it. He also uses his rehearsal time to watch others at work. In this way he can learn an immense amount about the building of a role and the techniques of acting.

The producer at rehearsal

The producer's job is to hold up a mirror to the actor, for unlike a painter or a writer, the actor cannot actually see what he is doing. As he becomes experienced he learns to see a remarkable amount even as he is doing it, but the producer is needed to keep on completing the picture for him. Many actors like to lope around the stage instead of walking and holding themselves straight. They may prefer to take tiny little trots around the stage when they are supposed to be striding manfully. Very often actors believe that they are doing one thing when they are in fact doing the opposite. The producer's job is to keep them informed of the reality. The producer must never allow an actor to appear ridiculous in front of an audience. The producer does not have to coin witty phrases to describe what the actor is doing. Quite often all that is necessary is to demonstrate with slight exaggeration what you want the actor to do. If you want a strong, powerful walk, demonstrate it. If you want perfectly erect carriage, demonstrate that too. At the same time make it clear that such things as listening to someone without fidgeting, walking well, and standing up straight are all part of the actor's technique and often take a long time to master. It is techniques such as these, by the way, which are so important to a production and which do not suddenly appear with any amount of improvising or sitting around talking. They need to be dealt with in direct relation to actual performances in actual productions.

Talking about the play

Rehearsal time does not have to be limited entirely to going over the play itself, with the actors on the stage working on the lines and the moves. Many producers regard this part of the job as only the last phase in a complex operation. In this as in any other aspect of theatrecraft you have to work out your own salvation. You may find that you can waste a tremendous amount of time getting ready for the play, only to find that you do not then have enough time to produce it effectively. You may perhaps decide that the most important thing in a production is that the actors should know exactly what they have to do at each moment of the performance, and that to reach this stage they need to have rehearsed very frequently and very thoroughly each moment of the play. Other producers do not like to work in this way, and even prefer their actors to improvise at the performance. This is up to the producer. All producers, however, should spend a certain amount of time talking about the play with the company. You must certainly do this when it is likely to help the actor to overcome his difficulties. You should also, of course, talk freely about the play to help the actors understand each dramatic situation in the play with regard to its psychological content, and its social and historical setting. In addition to this, some producers set aside certain rehearsals at regular intervals for the actors to sit down and talk about the play. They discuss its meaning, the various characters, and the performances. They hold a kind of 'teach-in' at which everybody is encouraged to air their views on every aspect of the production. In this way presumably everyone becomes involved in the production in a very full way and benefits from each other's opinions. On the other hand, such sessions can be highly demoralising, and some producers feel that the good results which are liable to come from this kind of talking, will come much more easily and with much less time spent, from an ordinary rehearsal and from talking casually to the various members of the company. It is certainly possible to spend too much time talking and this can bore and depress a company. Another technique which can be very useful is for the company to question each player in turn as to the character he is playing. He may be asked about the background of the character, how he was brought up, what he believes in, what he looks for in life, what he likes and what he dislikes. In this way the actors make each other think very clearly about their own roles, and about each other's.

Work on voice and speech

It is a good idea to set aside some time at rehearsals for work on voice and speech. Give a few simple exercises to the whole cast. The best type of voice work is not usually done where you ask the company to repeat vocal exercises as such, but where you ask them to use the exercises in some kind of improvisation. They will then perform the exercise with much more relish and enthusiasm. For instance, the most elementary speech exercise consists of taking each consonant in turn and articulating it in combination with various vowel sounds:

bar, bore, boo, bore, bar, bay, bee, bay.

The words are articulated carefully to get the full value of the vowel sound and they are practised until the actor can articulate each one precisely and in rapid succession. Then the consonant is changed to the hard C and then to D and so on right down the alphabet. In this way one exercises the vowels and consonants together. But once the company knows the exercise, use the exercise in different contexts. Use it as a vocal warming-up exercise before the rehearsal begins. Or ask them to improvise a cocktail party or a street market at which people speak not in words but in '*bar, bore, boo, bore*' and '*car, core, coo, core*' and so on. In this way they start to use tone and pitch and rhythm of speech to achieve what is normally left all too lazily to the words themselves. The actors begin to experiment with the possibilities of voice and sound. To develop a further sensitivity for careful articulation and tone, rhythm and pitch, get the company to improvise an opera, perhaps using a mock foreign language and such odds and ends of a foreign language as they happen to possess. Providing that you explain what you are doing all this for, you will help them to develop a greater awareness of voice and speech, and a greater vocal sensitivity.

Very often, when actors become interested for the very first time in speaking clearly and precisely, they fall into an extreme precision that is slightly ridiculous. The mistake usually made is either to hit the consonants too hard, or to over-emphasise what should be weak or small vowel sounds. In the first case the mistake must simply be pointed out to the actor until he stops doing it. In the second case the root of the problem is usually that the actor is unaware of what in phonetics is called the 'neutral' vowel sound. It is an ignorance of this sound which often makes even the most gifted foreign speaker of English sound a shade absurd. The neutral vowel sound occurs in so many English words as, for example, dis*a*ppear, beaut*i*ful, applic*a*nt, man*or*, col*our*, and is liable to appear in any combination of vowels. The spelling is no indication of whether it is present. In all the examples just given it will be noticed that the letters underlined are never stressed in pronunciation but are almost dropped as one speaks the word and that the sound made is exactly the same in each case despite the differences in spelling. This is called the 'neutral' vowel sound. A temptation by elocutionists to over-stress the neutral has to be guarded against very carefully. It is not a bad idea, once an actor has become aware of its existence, for him to go through a longish piece of prose, perhaps an extract from the play, marking down all the points where the neutral is used. The neutral is also used very commonly with the definite and indefinite articles ('the', 'a', and 'an') and with the monosyllabic prepositions and conjunctions such as 'and', 'but', 'to', 'of' and 'at'. But you may not necessarily use the neutral all the time with the same word—you may for instance want to stress a word on one occasion but not on another.

It must be brought home to the actor that despite the rather doubtful example of BBC news readers, whose English accent is often anything but standard, it is not good speech to turn the neutral vowel sound into long vowels. It is not good English to say 'A (as in bay) cup of (as in hot) tea'. In fact both the 'a' and the 'o' sounds should be neutral.

Rehearsal work on the voice should also be the occasion for the producer to talk to his cast about the danger of falling inflections. Many actors bring all their sentences to a mournfully trailing conclusion in which the end of the sentence is often very difficult to hear. This reduces the actor's speech to a repetitive sing-song in which the voice goes up at the beginning of the sentence and then begins to fall with predictable regularity towards the end. Once you have made clear what is wrong to the actor himself, you may find it quite useful to add to your vocal exercises improvised scenes in which everybody has to go round talking in falling inflections. This will make the monotony of the habit very clear to everyone. Then reverse the process and make everyone talk in sentences which go up at the end instead of falling off. As a general principle, though not an unalterable one, all sentences should go up at the end instead of down, and the actor should regard the end of the sentence as more important than the beginning.

The other vocal fault that crops up regularly is that the actors pick up each other's pitch, rhythm and tone and thereby destroy the balance of their acting. The producer must be alert to this danger, which is for some reason much greater in serious drama than it is in comedy, and improvisations can be given at rehearsals to eradicate the fault. Ask one actor to start talking in, say, a very tragic tone and then get the other characters to talk about quite different things in the same tone. This will again help to bring home the sheer unreality of vocal uniformity.

Improvisation

There are many additional purposes for which improvisations may be used, such as to explore character, to enrich the actor's imaginative understanding of what he is doing, to develop acting with others instead of acting on one's own. You may for instance have two characters in the play who come on stage after having just made a long train journey together. Ask the actors to improvise what happened on the train. If a character refers to an event he witnessed off stage, ask the actor to describe the event in great detail. This technique can be used in many different ways, but do not run away with the idea that any amount of improvisation will reduce the time you need to work on the script itself.

Improvisations can also be used in one form or another as a warming-up exercise before rehearsals begin. Improvisations based on various kinds of crowd scene can be very useful for this, such as asking the company to watch a football match, or asking them all to go to a noisy party at which the neighbours break in to complain. Or it may be a good idea to start with a sing-song.

Taking rehearsal work outside school

Take advantage of any opportunity to take the company to places relevant to the play. This may include art galleries, professional productions, films, and places connected either with the events of the play or with the life of the playwright.

IX *Scenery*

Producers often act as their own scenic designers, especially where they have a simple but effective idea in their minds of what the setting should be. Quite often the scenic designer also designs the costumes, but this does not have to be the case, and sometimes the costumes are hired rather than specially designed.

Developing the ideas for a set

Generally the development of the designs, from initial conception to building the set, will follow a pattern such as this:

(i) Producer and designer exchange ideas.

(ii) Designer conceives basic ideas for designs.

(iii) Designer puts the ideas on to paper in the form of a coloured picture.

(iv) Designer works his ideas out in detail so that they will fit on to the actual stage which is going to be used.

(v) Designer prepares a ground plan of the set, on a scale of half an inch to a foot. The ground plan simply shows the set as viewed from above and placed on the stage. Since it is made to scale it enables the producer to work out precisely the limits of the acting areas, as well as enabling the stage management to mark out on the stage the exact placing of the scenery.

(vi) The designer shows both the picture of the set (the elevation) and the ground plan to the producer and together they make any alterations that may be necessary.

(vii) From the ground plan and the elevation the designer makes a model, usually on a scale of half an inch to a foot.

(viii) From the model, the ground plan and the elevation, the actual scenery is built and eventually set up on the stage.

Terms used in scenic design

Before we proceed to look at the various kinds of sets which can be used, it may be helpful to go quickly through the various terms employed:

Flats A flat rectangular piece of scenery, consisting of canvas stretched on a wooden frame. Flats are supported from behind by a brace and counter-weight, and can be tied to each other by a cleat and line. Scenery is painted on to the front of the flat.

Box-set A stage design in which the two sides and the back of the stage are hidden behind a combination of flats, the flats representing for example the three walls of a room.

Cyclorama The painted back wall of a stage, or a taut canvas hung across the back of a stage.

Borders Portions of curtains hung from the top of the stage to conceal the stage roof from the audience's view. Or, pieces of canvas scenery hung in the same fashion.

Wings Either narrow curtains hanging at the sides of the stage to conceal the sides from the audience's view, or pieces of canvas scenery standing in the same position and fulfilling the same function.

Proscenium The main arch at the front of the stage separating the stage from the auditorium.

Sight-lines The lines which mark off the maximum area of vision of the entire audience. If a set is well designed then the sight-lines will be such that everybody in the audience will be able to see all of the set and therefore all of the acting area, and nobody will be able to see into the wings. When you are working in a hall where you can re-arrange the seating, it is of course essential to let your designer know exactly how you will place the seats before he

attempts to design the sets.

Cut-out flats These are flats in which the top part is cut out to show the actual shape of the object it is representing, for example, the foliage of a tree. In the older kind of light entertainment, such as operetta and pantomime, cut-outs are often used as wings and borders.

Trucks This is the term for any kind of movable unit built on castors and which can be moved around the stage. Cut-out flats are sometimes designed on trucks and they can then be moved around the stage, or on and off the stage, without any difficulty, perhaps during the action of the play.

Three-dimensional units on trucks These are the most useful and effective of all stage scenery. They are units of scenery built on trucks and which can be turned around to reveal a new setting. See illustrations *15*, *16* and *17*.

Apron or forestage Any kind of addition to the stage, whether permanent or improvised, built in front of the proscenium.

Traverse curtains Curtains hanging midway down the stage, and which can be closed to conceal the back of the stage from the audience's view.

Backing A piece of scenery placed behind another piece, to give some kind of realistic backing; for example, a view of a street placed behind a hall window.

The different kinds of stage setting

(i) *The bare stage* can be used very effectively but this means that the producer has to concentrate all interest upon the actors, the lighting and the costumes.

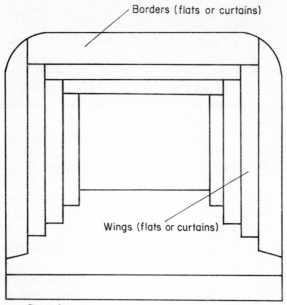

Borders (flats or curtains)

Wings (flats or curtains)

5   *Curtain set*

6   *Painted backcloth and cut-out wings*

(ii) *Curtain sets*   The same as (i) except for the addition of black curtains suspended in the wings and across the back of the stage. The colour does not have to be black—dark blue or grey can also be very effective—but avoid the use of oatmeal or pink for then the actors' faces tend to merge into the background. The same effect can be achieved with the use of flats instead of curtains (see illustration 5).

(iii) *Painted backcloth and cut-out wings*   This is the same as the previous design (ii) except that the stage has a painted backcloth at the back of it instead of a plain hanging curtain, and instead of the plain flats or curtains hanging in the wings, some kind of simple cut-out flats are used to represent some kind of actual scenery. See illustration 6. Notice that the ground plan for the two sets shown in illustrations 5 and 6 is exactly the same (see illustration 7).

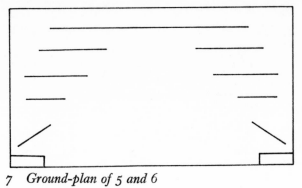

7　*Ground-plan of 5 and 6*

(iv) *Simple box-sets* Illustration *8* shows the ground plan of a simple box-set with wide walls slightly perspected to give an illusion of greater depth. Such a set would of course be suitable for a small stage. Notice that one should avoid plain straight walls on a stage, and in this illustration the walls are broken by the doors, the window and the fireplace. But usually where space permits it, the best way to break up long straight walls is by angling and recessing, as the later illustrations show.

(v) *Adapting one idea for the requirements of different stages* Illustration *9* shows the ground plan of a simple box-set depicting the interior of a cottage, designed for a stage which has plenty of width but very little depth. In illustration *10* the same basic design is used for a stage of equal width but greater depth, which allows for the set to be expanded and become much more interesting. The whole additional upstage area is mounted on a platform—say one foot high—to create a more interesting and varied set, and this is shown on the ground plan by a dotted line.

8　*Simple box-set*

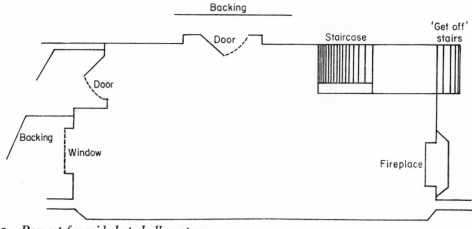

9　*Box-set for wide but shallow stage*

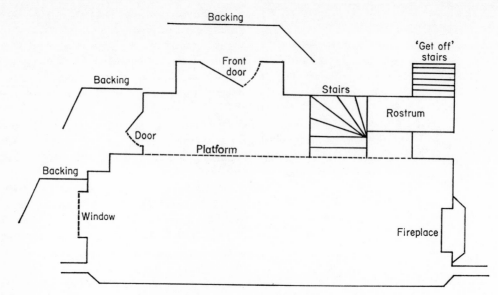

10   Box-set for wide and deep stage

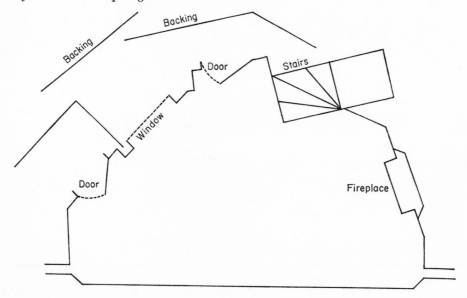

11   More interesting version of 10

Illustration *11* shows the same set angled in a rather more novel fashion and in a way which makes quite sure that all members of the audience can see all its details. Illustration *12* shows the same set adapted to a much narrower stage. Angling the walls in this way not only makes the set more interesting to look at but also allows much more wing space. Illustration *13* gives a bird's eye view picture of the set as originally shown in illustration *9* and upon which all the other three ground plans are mere variations.

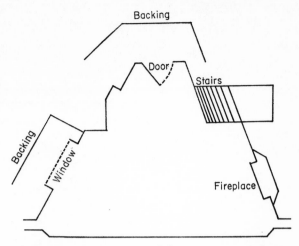

12   Box-set for narrow and deep stage

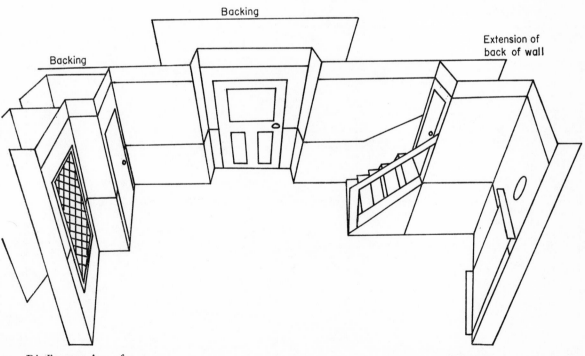

13   Bird's eye view of 9

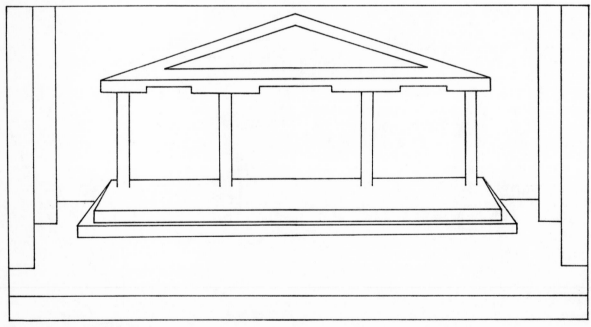

14   Simple stylised setting

(vi) *Cyclorama* used in combination with a single stylised setting—as shown in illustration *14*.

(vii) *Cyclorama* or backcloth in combination with various pieces of cut-out flats, and perhaps double-sided flats, placed on trucks. You might, for instance, have a cut-out of a church on one side of the stage and of a shop on the other. If you have them on trucks then you can wheel them about as you like without difficulty and perhaps the actors can move them around in the action of the play. Double-sided flats on trucks can be particularly useful.

(viii) *Three-dimensional units built on trucks* These can be revolved by the actors to reveal new settings (see illustrations *15*, *16* and *17*). Note that these units have to be bolted to the floor if they are to be stable, and have to be re-bolted every time they are re-positioned or re-angled. The actors themselves can revolve the sets, either in full light or perhaps with all lights taken out except for a light on the cyclorama. This creates an interesting visual effect as well as leaving the actors enough light for them to be able to see what they are doing.

(ix) If you have no carpenters to build your sets for you, then you can create very interesting stylised sets with various combinations of *steps, rostra and ramps* (see illustration *18*).

Two final overall comments may be made about scenic design:

(i) Do not be afraid to mix all the various styles of stage design to your own convenience.

(ii) The simpler your scenery, the better. Never ever use scenery which in any way holds up the action of the play. Never ever make your audience wait while you change the set, unless it is a wait of about ten seconds and the change is performed in front of the audience, along the lines suggested in the notes on three-dimensional units. Similarly, make quite sure that the scenery is suitable to the particular stage on which you are working. Does it take up too much space? Does it unduly restrict the movement of the actors? Here, again, simplicity is the greatest virtue.

15   *Three-dimensional units on trucks*

16   *Units in 15 revolved to create new setting*

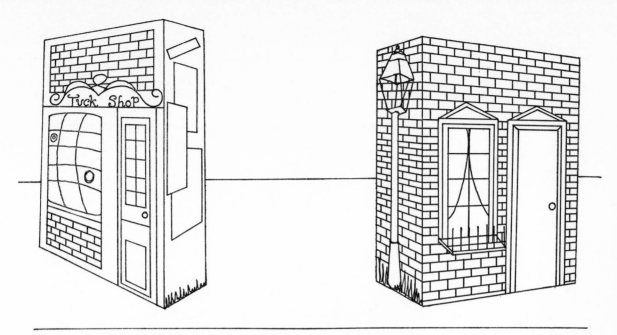

17   *The same units as in 15 and 16 re-angled*

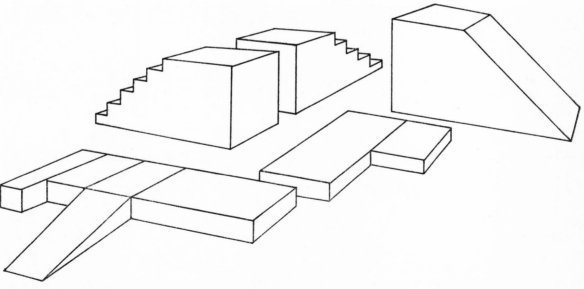

18   Rostra and steps

X *Lighting*

General principles

(i) The most common mistake in the planning of stage lighting is to think of it only as a means of lighting the set or the stage itself. Its purpose is chiefly to *light the actors* in such a way that they are fully visible to the audience and in such a way as to create the appropriate dramatic atmosphere.

(ii) The most satisfactory way to light actors is by 'directional lighting'. This consists of the use of spotlights in combination with a very sparing and judicious use of floodlights.

(iii) To light a play well it is not necessary to have a large number of lights to work with. A very good lighting plan can be devised with ten spots and a couple of floods.

(iv) In general, the centre and upstage areas of the stage are illuminated by lights hanging above (or standing on) the stage. The downstage area and fore-stage are illuminated by lights suspended from the front-of-house.

(v) Stage lights can either be suspended from bars or wall brackets, or supported on stands. Occasionally it is useful to put the stands themselves on boxes to achieve added height for the source of light.

The different kinds of stage lighting

There are two kinds:

Spotlights These illuminate a well-defined area. There are three kinds of spotlight:

(i) *Mirror-profile spot* (illustration *19*) This has a hard-edged beam. Different shapes can be placed in the gate between the reflector and the lens, and by this means any shape of spot can be produced, such as circular, semi-circular or oblong.

(ii) *Focus lantern* (illustration *20*) This does not give a small clear-cut spot, but lights a more

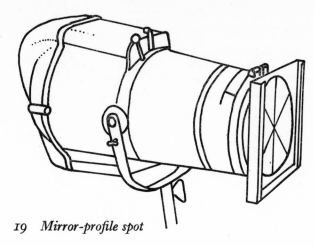

19   Mirror-profile spot

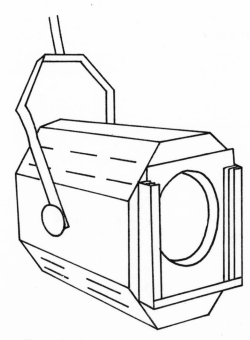

20   Focus Lantern

general area. It is in fact halfway between a spot and a flood.

(iii) *Fresnel spot* (illustration *21*) This produces an adjustable circular spot and it can therefore be used to illuminate a small or large area. The light is most intense at the centre of its beam and it is soft-edged. Of the three kinds of spotlight it is the most subtle in its effect and probably the most useful.

Floodlights These illuminate large areas, but they do not have a directional beam and therefore give diffuse lighting rather than specific lighting. Consequently one uses spotlights to light the actors, and floodlights are used either to light a backcloth or cyclorama, or to give an added 'lift' to a scene where bright illumination is called for. Floodlights may be either *single floods* (illustration *22*) or groups of floods encased in long rectangular boxes, in which case they are called *battens*. The commonest of these is *footlights*, but battens can also be used (and nowadays are more commonly used, since footlights are generally considered unnecessary) for hanging from a bar either on the main stage or just in front of the cyclorama (see illustration *23*).

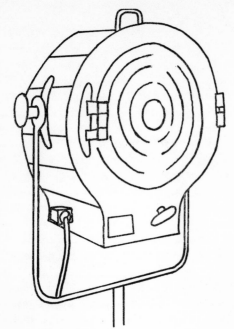

21   *Fresnel spot*

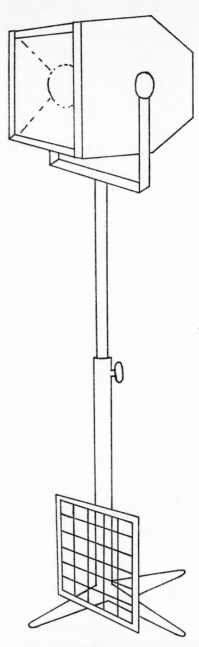

22   *Single flood*

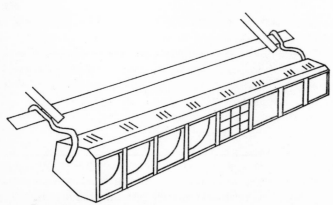

23   *Batten*

24　*Single spot directed at centre stage*

An approach to stage lighting

It may be helpful for the beginner to approach the problem of stage lighting in these simple stages:

(i) *Illuminating the actors with a single spotlight directed at the centre stage*　Illustration 24 shows two actors illuminated by one spotlight. This allows them to be seen but gives them little freedom of movement. Note that the light is hung from the centre of the Number One Spot Bar. This is the bar which hangs immediately behind the proscenium arch. When a light is hung from this bar it can of course only illuminate actors when

they are either centre stage or upstage. If such a light is aimed downstage then it has to be pointed straight downwards, in which case it merely lights up the tops of the actors' heads.

(ii) *Illuminating the actors with a small group of spotlights directed at the centre stage*　Illustration 25 shows the addition of two spots, hanging from stage left and stage right respectively of the Number One Spot Bar. Notice that the spots are so directed that their light overlaps. This has to be experimented with until an even spread of light is obtained. Notice also that the area illuminated is still centre stage.

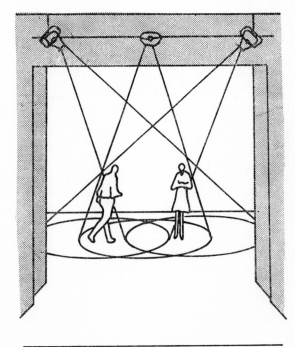

25　*Group of spots directed at centre stage*

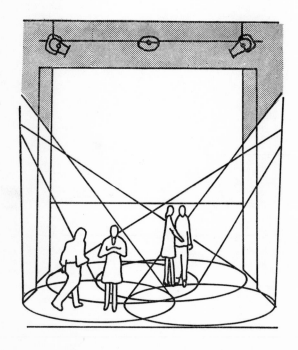

26   *Lighting the downstage*

(iii) *Illuminating the actors in the downstage area with spotlights hanging from the front-of-house* Illustration 26 shows the illumination of the downstage area by the use of two pairs of spots suspended from either side of the front-of-house. If you add to this the lights suspended from the Number One Spot Bar as shown in illustration 25, you will have the whole acting area fairly well covered. This is shown in illustration 27. Note that these illustrations demonstrate what can be done with limited resources on a fairly small stage. Obviously, the wider and deeper the stage, the more lighting will be needed to cover it.

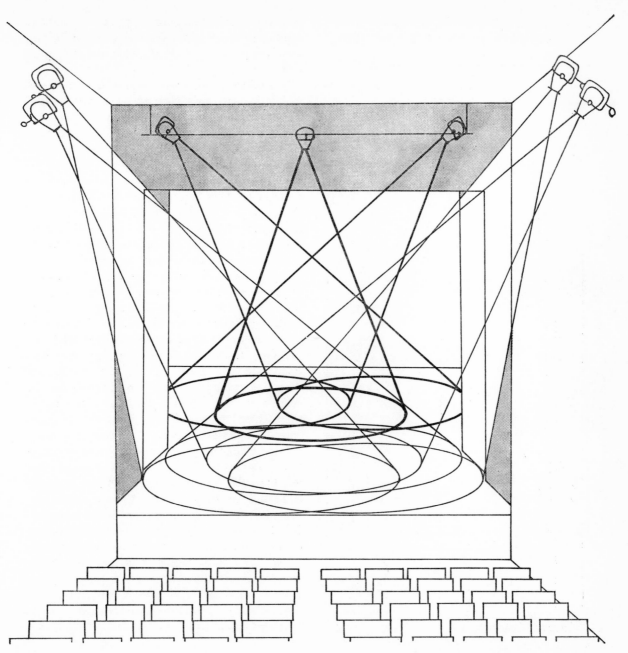

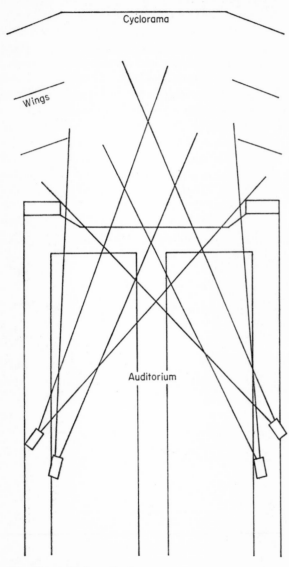

28   Ground plan of 26

Illustration *28* is a ground plan of the lighting used in illustration *26*. Ground plans of lighting show the producer precisely what areas the lights will cover.

(iv) *Lighting the actors on the fore-stage area* Much the same principle applies as with lighting the downstage area. Use a couple of spots at each side of the front-of-house, and a large spot from the centre of the hall, hanging either from a bar or from a balcony. If you have neither bar nor balcony you can still cover the fore-stage quite adequately from the sides. Illustration *29* shows a ground plan for lighting the apron. Spotlights which hang or stand at the side of the front-of-house should be at least 10 feet from the proscenium arch and at least 14 feet high.

(v) *Lighting the actors on the upstage area* If you use the upstage area for acting purposes then you will probably need some light in addition to the light given in the illustrations. This can be achieved simply by adding two spots to the Number One Spot Bar hanging respectively one-third and two-thirds of the way across, and with their beams crossing and aimed at the up-stage area. Alternatively you may prefer to use these spots to add further light to the centre stage or downstage area.

(vi) *Lighting the cyclorama* If you are using the cyclorama to create an illusion of sky the best way to do this is by hanging a set of batten lighting from the top of the stage at least 3 feet from the cyclorama, using two or three lengths of 6 feet each, and placing the same amount along the floor in front of the cyclorama and at the same distance. (If your stage is quite a small one then you can create the same effect with a couple of individual floods.) If your stage is equipped with footlights, then this is a better use for them than it is to leave them in front of the main curtain, for you

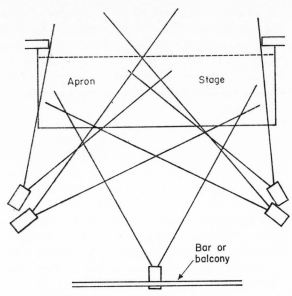

29 *Lighting the apron*

will be able to light your actors quite effectively with spots and without using the footlights at all. When you use battens for lighting the cyclorama you should use wide-angle reflectors in each compartment. If your battens are so circuited that three or four different colours can be used separately, then use one circuit of open white, one circuit of steel (number 17 filter) and one circuit of deep blue (number 20) and mix them until you get the colour that you want.

(vii) *Lighting the backings* Many stage sets have backings. These are views seen through, say, windows or doors. They can consist of a painted backcloth, or a painted flat, or a portion of the cyclorama. These have to be lit quite independently of the rest of the stage. Flood lighting is usually the simplest answer, using either single floods or battens (see illustration 30).

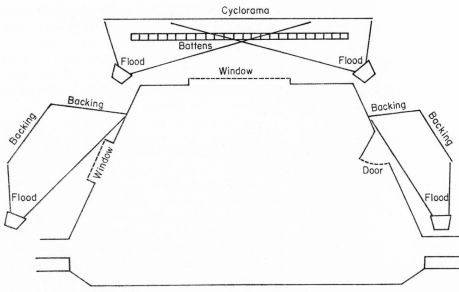

30 *Lighting the backings*

(viii) *Use of colour filters* Stage lighting is helped by the use of different colour filters, in the form of gelatine or plastic sheets, which can be fitted in front of spots and floods. These have standard names and numbers. There are about sixty different colours but the most useful are:

Number 3   straw
Number 17   steel blue
Number 18   light blue
Number 50   pale yellow
Number 52   pale gold
Number 53   pale salmon
Number 54   pale rose

A few hints may be given about the use of colour filters. A mixing of 50, 52, 53 and 54 will usually give the right kind of balance to the acting area. As a rule keep off the deep colours or the hot colours such as purple, orange or red. Use 17—steel blue—for hard brightness or moonlight. If you want the real colour of costumes to be brought out, only use the palest colour filters, otherwise the colours will disappear into an overall muddiness.

Working out the lighting

Designing the lighting for a show is usually done in the initial stages of a production. Very obviously, if you are lighting a straightforward comedy, in which all the action takes place in the drawing-room in the daytime, then you will need very cheerful lighting throughout, though you may have to leave a couple of spots in reserve if, say, you are doing a play which in the last act switches to a sunlit garden. When you come to plays whose location and mood vary constantly, you can of course experiment much more freely.

Remember that in lighting, as in anything else on the stage, contrast is the key word. Vary your lighting at every plausible opportunity. Do not start the play with all the lights you have, unless this is essential. Vary also the areas which you illuminate. It can be most effective, for instance, to depict the approach of night by slowly fading the lights on the upstage and centre areas until just the apron or downstage areas are left illuminated. This is more effective than simply dimming everything. Remember also that you can contrast different intensities of light, as well as contrasting total blackout and light. If you are lighting a revue or music hall, then you may find it very useful to have one spot which is manually directed in the course of the show to follow specific performers. Here, again, you should vary your lighting from one number to the next.

Once the lighting designs have been tentatively agreed upon, the designer usually gives the producer the ground plans of the lighting, so that the producer can see precisely the areas of light which the designs will create.

Setting up the lights

Each spot and each flood has to be set separately. The lighting director will usually need three assistants. The first assistant positions the light, the second assistant sits at the switch board, and the third assistant moves across the stage in the various areas of light so that the lighting director can see whether the lights are in the right position and at the right angle. Colour filters are placed inside each light as soon as it is satisfactorily positioned. Usually the first lights to be set are those on the Number One Spot Bar (i.e. behind the proscenium arch) followed by those on the Number Two Spot Bar (i.e. the bar hanging across the centre of the stage, if you have one) and then the front-of-house lights are fixed. Lights on the cyclorama and the lights on the backings are left until last. Each light is positioned individually, first against a background of complete blackness and then in conjunction with the other lights. The process is normally a lengthy one and you often need to do a lot of re-arranging before the lights can be permanently fixed.

Operating the lights

This can be done in two ways:

(i) The lighting director sits out front, at the back of the hall, where he has his own control box from which he controls all the stage lighting and the front-of-house lights as well. In this case he simply tells his assistants when to change the lights. Alternatively, where the lighting controls are back-stage, the designer may still have a box in the front-of-house from which he watches the action of the play, and from which he is connected by inter-com. with his staff back-stage.

(ii) All the lighting equipment is back-stage and so are the director and his assistants.

Usually the lighting director gives his assistants the cues for the changes of lighting in two stages. First he gives the cue 'Get ready for Number 8' a minute or so before the Number 8 lighting cue is actually imminent, and then he gives the cue 'Go Number 8' at the appropriate moment. All lighting cues are numbered, so that the assistants who actually operate the lights simply follow the list of numbers with the details of the operations to be performed at each lighting cue.

XI *Rehearsals: Later Stages*

The producer

In the last phase of rehearsals the producer allows his actors to run through whole acts and sometimes the entire play, without any interruption, so that they can see clearly the relationship of each part of the play to the whole, and so that they can get a flow on their performances. This leads up to the dress rehearsals and the actual performances. After the run-through the actors gather on stage and the producer gives them his notes on what they have just done. If the producer does not allow his actors these runs-through, or if he fails to get to the point where they can have runs-through until the last week of rehearsal, then the company will never have that ease and polish which comes from having been through the play in full quite a number of times before the audience arrives. In this event, the producer is encouraging nervousness and panic among his actors, because the thought that keeps most

actors going when they are about to appear on stage is the fact that they know exactly what they have to do.

The producer's notes, given after each rehearsal, should be brief, and as far as possible should not involve setting out on any new ground. This does not mean that you should never under any circumstances change a single detail of a production in the closing period of rehearsals, for very often the producer or some one else in the company sees at the last minute a brilliant new idea which simply has to be incorporated. But never make a policy of this. As often as not, even the most brilliant ideas, when they are introduced at the last moment never really work because the company have not acquired real familiarity with them. It is when the production is suddenly changed in this way that actors are most likely to forget their lines on stage.

The producer must always remember that as far as the actor is concerned he is the only person who can see what the audience is going to see. The actor relies upon the producer, therefore, to point out the virtues and deficiencies of what he is doing. Some producers wax eloquent at rehearsals over the virtues of particular players, and this is fine provided other actors also have their virtues pointed out to them. There is nothing more demoralising than acting in a play in which the producer reserves all his praise for one or two players. Every actor should receive praise and criticism, especially in the note-giving sessions. Make a particular point of praising those who do the unsensational but very important things—such as standing still while others are talking. Also, where you find something to criticise, find something to praise as well. Never presume that an actor knows his own qualities, or that because he is a good actor he also has plenty of confidence. If an actor makes a magnificent entrance, or if, say, he does a superb bow, full of just the panache that you want, then do not be afraid to tell the actor how well he enters, or how well he bows. Otherwise you will find, especially with inexperienced actors, that they will quite suddenly, perhaps at an actual performance, stop doing the particular little detail that you most enjoyed and were most anxious for them to repeat.

You may perhaps find that some actors start to change everything they do as they get nearer to the actual performances. The fault may in fact lie with the producer. Many young actors simply do not realise that the purpose of rehearsals is that the actors do literally 'rehearse'—meaning that they prepare in exact detail for what they will do at a performance. They look upon rehearsals as a kind of try-out for the real thing, and consider that they can reject whatever they fancy once the rehearsals are over. In a sense, of course, the rehearsal is a try-out, but there should be no radical departure from the set moves and inter-pretation during the closing stages of rehearsals, unless the actor consults the producer before making an experiment and gets his approval. The producer must make it clear from the start that the object is to consolidate the production by the time the company gets to the point of having a run-through, so that everyone can fall into the rhythm of the production and become fully familiar with it, and know exactly what they are doing.

The actor

The final rehearsals are the time when the actor puts together all the work he has done on a production. He may at this time find quite unexpected difficulties. He may very well find that while he can cope in individual scenes with the role he is playing, to sustain it through an entire play is almost beyond him. This will probably not be the case if he is playing a relatively minor character, but for the young actor who finds himself in a leading role, in which he has to be on stage for perhaps two hours or more, the sudden realisation that the performances are imminent can be quite terrifying. The answer is that, in fact, to play a leading role in a major production is indeed terrifying. It takes cheek, nerve and daring, as well as talent and hard work. There is all the difference in the world between playing a character who goes on, say, three separate times in the course of the play, leaving the stage on each occasion after about five minutes, and playing the character who remains on stage all the way through everybody else's exits and entrances, and who is still on stage when all the other actors are merrily chatting away in their dressing-room. Most of us could cope more or less successfully with a small role, but very few of us would even dare to play a major role. The longer one remains on stage, the more confidence one needs, the more experience, the more energy and the more nerve. For the longer the part, the longer the time the audience has to discover one's shortcomings, to study one's defects and idiosyncrasies. It is not by accident that in the professional theatre the leading players usually earn substantially more than the supporting players, for their job is by definition a much harder one. So the young actor who is taking a major role in the production may quite likely find that he is either depressed or exhausted, or both, by the rehearsals, especially when it comes to complete runs-through of the entire play. In general all actors, if they are working to their maximum, should find all rehearsals and all performances exhausting.

A further point may be made about last-minute difficulties. Many actors create unnecessary problems for themselves by trying to evoke emotional responses in themselves which simply cannot be evoked either at all or at least not at every rehearsal and performance. Such actors may suddenly find at the dress rehearsal that they cannot 'feel' the kind of involvement that they felt at the previous runs-through. Another form of the same problem is the actor who just cannot convince himself, when he has to parade across the stage, that he is a mighty monarch or the town's most delinquent juvenile. In cases such as these, the actor should attempt, just as an experiment, not to '*believe*' in what he is doing, nor to '*convince*' himself, but to give the performance, or at least the part of it that he finds difficult, as if he were giving a '*demonstration*' to the audience. In other words, he stops thinking about his own response to what he is doing,

and thinks instead of creating vividly for the audience the sort of drama that the playwright has created. Instead of trying to 'be' the character, he gives an impressionistic display, so that the actor is inwardly saying to the audience, 'I am not in fact the hero of this play, leading my regiment to victory over the enemy, but I am showing you roughly how I think the character would behave in such circumstances'. In short, the actor imitates the producer when he stands up to demonstrate to the actor what he wants. Many good performers lose heart quite unnecessarily because they become obsessed with what they think they are feeling, or should be feeling.

Also, actors should be careful never to discourage one another. They can do this in a variety of ways, for example, by giggling at the back of the hall while other actors are rehearsing, by not being punctual, by expressing no enthusiasm for the play, or by not learning their lines until the latest possible moment. All the members of a company should consciously attempt to keep each other confident and optimistic. Where an actor has a criticism to make, then there should be opportunities for the actor to voice his criticism in front of the producer, so that the producer can either reject it or act upon it. There may perhaps be specific times at some rehearsals for all the actors to discuss the play, or the practice may be for actors to discuss their criticisms with the producer quite privately after the rehearsal. In any event the actor must have every opportunity to voice his opinions, but he must in his turn accept the overall responsibility of the producer to make his own decisions, and the actor must then be prepared to let his criticism drop. Actors may often need to be reminded, especially where they have not worked before on a large production, that they need each other's goodwill just as much as they need an audience. Also, strangely enough, producers need the goodwill and encouragement of their actors, just as much as actors need the goodwill and encouragement of their producer. If the producer places himself at a mighty distance from his players, then he is of course unlikely to receive much encouragement from them. He is also unlikely to achieve anything very remarkable in the way of production.

The assistant producer

In addition to taking some rehearsals on the producer's behalf, he should make it his personal responsibility to see that understudies know their parts, and are given a fair amount of rehearsal time. If you follow the usual practice of having the actors understudy each other (rather than having understudies who are not in the company at all) then you will find that the actor improves tremendously as a result of working on the role he is understudying, provided of course that he is given enough rehearsals. It is a good idea, in addition to having special understudy rehearsals, to let different understudies take over at different rehearsals, so that the understudy has a chance to play scenes with the other principal players.

XII *Stage Management*

At rehearsals

The stage manager is responsible for:

(i) Making sure that the stage or hall is ready for the actors to proceed with the rehearsal. Where you use an acting area that is not already marked out for you, such as a stage extension which will not be erected until the week before the performances, then the stage manager should mark out this area for the actors at rehearsal, either in chalk or in tape tacked to the floor. This will probably have to be removed after each rehearsal. The stage manager should also mark the boundaries of the scenery in this way, including the position of doors. This is necessary in order that the actors can rehearse in the same space which they will eventually perform in. Otherwise the actors either exaggerate or underestimate the amount of space they will be given and are therefore completely thrown when it comes to performances.

(ii) Marking his script with every move that the producer gives to the actor. This need only be in shorthand form (e.g. U.L. for Up Left). Where there are a lot of such moves, it is best, as with the producer's copy, to number the moves and to insert blank pages with the details of each move. The marking of moves includes noting down the parts of the stage from which characters enter and exit. At a later point, when the lighting designer has produced his lighting plot, the stage manager also marks down in his script the points at which the lighting changes. The stage manager's script therefore becomes a complete record of every aspect of the production, so that he can see, when it comes to dress rehearsal and performance, exactly how the production is intended to function.

(iii) Setting out suitable substitute furniture and providing suitable substitute props for each rehearsal, so that the rehearsal can proceed as far as possible like a real performance. Sometimes, of course, the same props and furniture which will be used at the performances will also be used at rehearsal.

(iv) If the producer wants a prompter then this is normally the stage manager's job. It is often a very good idea to have a prompter at the early rehearsals only, when this can help the actors to keep some kind of flow at the run-through of scenes, but later the prompter is sometimes best withdrawn. You do not have to have a prompter at performances. You can encourage your actors to help each other out when they get into difficulties, and to improvise. If you do have a prompter this can encourage actors to depend on him instead of upon themselves and each other. There is no hard and fast rule in this matter, and obviously you should discuss this with your cast before reaching any decision.

At dress rehearsals and performances

At this point the stage manager takes over the responsibility for the production from the producer himself. The stage manager is responsible for co-ordinating every aspect of the production at the dress rehearsals and performances:

(i) The manager and his assistants (usually about five) prepare the stage for the performance. This means that they set up the scenery, prepare for any changes of scenery, and mark clearly on the stage exactly where scenery has to be placed. This marking is usually done with washable paint. In this way the stage management can see very clearly where a piece of scenery goes, even though it may have to be put into position with great speed in a scene-change. The stage manager must also mark the points on the stage at which furniture has to be placed in position. Different colours of paint are used for these markings, and they must be made with the collaboration of the producer, so that the precise position where, say, a small stool is placed for use in scene three, can be exactly fixed.

(ii) The stage manager delegates responsibility for props to one of his assistants. The assistant has not only to ensure that all props are available before each performance, but must also see to it that each prop is in its right place at the right time. If, for instance, an actor has to walk on carrying a gun, then the assistant must see to it that the actor is given the gun a reasonable time before he goes on with it. This will also mean making sure that props are in place before each scene begins. If the list of props is a complicated one, then you may find it helpful to have a second props man so that you can have one man in charge on each side of the stage.

(iii) The stage manager is responsible for calling the actors at the beginning of each performance. Usually it is adequate to call them at 15 minutes before the performance is due to begin, at 5 minutes (when all actors in the first scene should report on stage) and then to send out an assistant with the news for the remainder of the company that the curtain has just gone up. It is up to the producer to decide whether he wants the actors to receive further individual calls in the course of the play. In the professional theatre this practice is rapidly going out of fashion and the stage manager may make no further calls after 'Curtain Up' except to call the actors on stage at the end of intervals. Much depends in school productions on the siting of the dressing-rooms, and whether there is plenty of wing space where actors can wait before they make their entrances. If the stage manager does in fact have to call each actor for each entrance, then he must mark clearly in his script the points where each actor should be warned that his entrance is imminent. This is usually about 5 minutes before he actually has to enter. The manager will need an assistant whose job it is to call the actors and to do nothing else.

(iv) If you decide to have a prompter then this should be the stage manager himself. Do not have some one who has only just walked into the production. He will not know the play well enough to prompt efficiently and economically.

(v) The stage manager controls the curtains. He decides when the stage, the actors, the lighting, and the front-of-house are ready for the curtain to go up. He also controls the lowering of the curtain and the taking of curtain calls. This means that the stage manager must have liaison with the lighting director so that house lights go down when the stage manager so orders, and he must also have liaison with the front-of-house manager. You must either have an inter-com. connecting the front-of-house manager with the stage manager, or else you should use a messenger service. Either way, the stage manager must not allow the curtain to go up without first checking that the front-of-house, the lighting director, and the actors in the opening scene, are all ready.

(vi) The stage manager is responsible for all sound effects, and cues for these must be marked in his script. If there are a lot of these then one assistant will be placed in charge of all of them.

Instruction sheets

Stage management is sometimes so complex that it is a good idea for the stage manager and the producer to work out a 'book' of all the various stage management instructions. This is typed out and copies are given to all the members of the stage management and to any actors connected with stage management. Additional copies are pinned to walls around the backstage area. This book will sometimes run to as many as a dozen pages, at other times it may be far less. It lists in chronological sequence everything that has to be done by the stage management and includes not only *what* must be done, but also *when* and *by whom*. An example of the first page of such a book would be rather like this:

PRIOR TO CURTAIN UP
John Warn actors 15 minutes before show commences.
Bill Check props list, collecting all props in wings Right before placing all props in position for scene one.
(Check from props list at back of book.)
John and Bob Check scenery set for scene one. John check furniture is in place from furniture list at back of book.
John Warn lighting director 5 minutes to curtain up.
Warn actors.
Check with f.o.h. that all is ready.
Call 'Go' to lighting director at 8 p.m. sharp, and to Bob (curtain operator).

DURING SCENE ONE
Bill Be ready Right to give Kay her bag for second entrance
Tom Ring bell at cue 'I must go now. . . . It's dinner time'
Bill Get plates, knives and forks ready to put on table during first scene change.
Bob Close traverse curtains on cue from Kay 'Come again. The same time tomorrow'.

DURING SCENE CHANGE AT END OF SCENE ONE
(while play continues in front of traverse)

John and Bob Revolve unit to cover lines marked in red.

Bob Strike (i.e. remove) two chairs.

Harry Strike wash stand and hat stand.

John Set two chairs at table, setting on green circular markings.

Bill Set glasses and decanter.

In this way everybody can see exactly what he has to do, from the beginning of a performance down to its end. You can even have a note of jobs that have to be done after the show and before the stage can be left. Include everybody on this list who has any job connected with the stage management. Each member of the stage management should receive a fresh copy of the 'book' for each performance so that he can cross off each item as it comes up. The 'book' can easily be run off on the school duplicating machine.

XIII *Programmes and Publicity*

Programmes

(i) These should introduce the play to the audience. Some kind of note is necessary to give the audience the right kind of expectation. If your play is a combination of music hall and social commentary, then say so, and if you need some kind of analogy with other plays or entertainments to make this clear, then do not be afraid of making the analogy. Never presume that your audience is as sophisticated as you are. You will inevitably have much more knowledge of the particular play you are presenting than will most of your audience. Also, school audiences are notoriously shy and afraid of doing the wrong thing. Whole regiments of aunts and uncles may refrain from laughing at an outrageous comedy unless they are assured that it is in fact an outrageous comedy. You might almost say that you need a programme to tell the audience what you are going to do, and then all you need is a good enough production actually to do it. You may perhaps consider using your programmes as tickets, or alternatively including the price of the programmes in the ticket-money, so that you give the programmes away at the performance as opposed to selling them. This is sometimes the only way of ensuring that all your audience sees a programme.

A recent touring production of *Twelfth Night*, aimed particularly at school audiences, struck exactly the right note by prefacing the performances with a specially written introduction in which each character in turn was presented to the audience. And then the play began. This policy can also be carried into the writing of the programme.

(ii) List the cast and the scenes in such a way as to make a large number of characters and complicated scene changes very clear to the audience. Characters should not necessarily be placed in order of appearance. It may be more convenient to list them in groups, for example:

Jack Smith

His family:
    Uncle Harry
    Aunt Flo
    Grandma
    Cousin Willy

His friends:
    Jack
    Bill
    Percy

His enemies:
    Mack
    Mary

Sometimes the characters change with each scene, in which case the cast list should become part of the synopsis of scenes.

(iii) List all people who have contributed to the production.

(iv) Include various follow-up information. If, for example, you have done a play like *Left Handed Liberty* then list any other of Arden's plays which can be obtained in the school library and perhaps in the local library as well. Give also the titles of any books which can be obtained which deal historically with the same material. Perhaps include a short essay written by someone in the company, or perhaps by an independent but interested pupil, that provokes readers to thinking further about what they have just seen.

(v) Include information on the Drama Club, the way it works, what kind of activities it does when not preparing for major productions, and lists of past productions.

(vi) The programme should be so designed, in terms of cover design, paper used, and the general layout of its contents, as to convey very vividly the atmosphere of the production. The art department of your school should have a field day on the planning of the programme. Cover designs do not have to be complex, but they should usually convey a symbolic or representational image of something that is fundamental to the play. If in addition to the programmes you are also going to use posters and perhaps handbills as well, then it is often a good idea to have a single motif run through the designs. If you are printing your programmes at the school then you may perhaps use the duplicator for the inside pages and silk-screen process printing for the cover. Some schools have the cover produced on coloured paper by the school and the editorial pages printed on white paper by professional printers.

Handbills

A good set of handbills can be most useful. A handbill should be a fairly small single sheet of paper with information on both sides. Always use coloured paper. The handbill announces the play and introduces it, and should be so written as to whet the appetite of the reader. A handbill which simply names the play is of limited value, but a handbill which says enough about it to interest complete outsiders is most valuable. Usually one side of the handbill introduces the play with some information, while the other side simply announces it. If you send them to a professional printer, then 1,000 handbills will cost around £10. Many schools print their own, and this is sometimes better because it is then possible to incorporate some kind of design into the announcement side. (If you ask the printers to include a design you will increase the cost very significantly.) The handbills can be distributed among pupils, among other schools, local newspapers, and among members of the public to whom pupils are trying to sell tickets.

Writing the content of the handbill can be the responsibility of the assistant producer or the production manager. Alternatively it can be used as a class-room exercise and as a means of introducing the play to the pupils.

Posters

The design of posters is sometimes entrusted to those pupils who are working with the scenic designer. Another equally good policy is to ask pupils in art classes to study the play and prepare their own posters for it, perhaps calling in at some of the rehearsals and talking to the producer and the players. The school then uses the best of these (in other words, a mixed selection) as the actual posters for the production. This brings a much wider range of pupils into an active involvement with the production, and that of course is the purpose of the whole project.

XIV *Front-of-House*

The front-of-house manager is responsible for:

(i) *Drawing up the seating plan* This must be done in collaboration with the producer, and care must be taken that no one in the audience has to sit in such a position that a part of the acting area is permanently blocked from his vision. Some producers are notoriously careless on this point and seem to think nothing of condemning a major part of the audience to an evening of frustration. Everyone who pays to see the show, or is invited to do so, should have a good seat, where it is possible to see all the acting area all the time. If the hall is a very big one, designed to accommodate 1,000 pupils or more at morning assembly, then you should avoid having any part of the audience at the opposite end of the hall to the stage. This is another good reason for having flexible staging as it enables you to bring the acting area right out into the hall, so that the entire audience can be near to the action of the play. To provide for an audience of 500 at five performances is usually enough. At all events you should try to let your company give at least five performances, for with less than this they will not experience the pleasure and the excitement of really becoming used to acting with audiences. You may be able to have a special matinee to which local old age pensioners or other local groups are invited as guests. All this will not only be a pleasant gesture on the part of the school, but also add to the enjoyment of the company.

(ii) *Arranging for the sale of tickets prior to the performance* Where your school does not have a great tradition of school plays then you may find it necessary to keep the sale of tickets going for quite a long period before the performances. Number your tickets in both row and seat. Audiences always like to know beforehand exactly where they will be sitting. The usual practice is for the front-of-house manager to draw up a seating plan for each performance and to mark off on the plan each seat as it is sold. Among the various ways of promoting ticket sales one of the most useful is to establish a tradition of exchange visits with nearby schools on the occasion of their respective school plays.

(iii) *Sale of tickets and programmes at the performance* If you sell the programmes, you will find that you very seldom sell half as many as you expect. Often no more than one fifth of an audience actually buy individual programmes.

(iv) *Provision of interval refreshments* If this is well organised a very considerable profit can be made towards meeting the expenses of the production.

(v) *Running the front-of-house during and prior to the performance* This means that the manager must be in contact with the stage manager either by messenger or by inter-com., so that the curtain does not go up until the front-of-house is ready i.e. the audience is seated, all doors are closed, and there is no light coming in from the foyer or from any entrances or windows. The manager must stay on duty throughout the performance to make sure that no doors are suddenly opened and left open, or that no curtains over doors are suddenly pulled aside and not closed again. He must also ensure that all exits are left clear throughout the performance.

XV *Make-up*

Stage make-up and school plays

When stage make-up is used in the professional theatre it has two distinct purposes: to reveal, and to conceal.

When stage make-up is used in school productions it should be used for one purpose only: to reveal. It is a common mistake to believe that you can take a school actor, and change the age and character of his face by the skilful use of make-up. The results are usually grotesque, and for various reasons:

(i) The whole basis of making-up the face of a professional actor is that you use shading and highlighting to emphasise or conceal the characteristics that the face already possesses. Hence if an actor of 40 is playing a character of 80 he takes the lines and folds of skin that are already appearing and emphasises them with his make-up. With the face of a 14 year old, or even an 18 year old, these lines are simply not present. The skin is smooth and taut, the flesh has not yet begun to sag, and no amount of stage make-up will ever conceal the fact. The converse also applies. You cannot take the face of an old person and take away the folds of flesh and the lines of the skin simply by the application of sticks of make-up. Once again the result is grotesque.

(ii) It is extremely difficult for an actor to live up to his make-up if the make-up is a very distinctive one. This is why professional actors always apply their own make-up and indeed become highly accomplished make-up artists. They know exactly what they are doing when they apply their make-up and know whether or not it is blending with their performance.

(iii) The whole purpose of stage make-up, with a few special exceptions, is that it should look as though the person is not in fact made-up. The more you attempt to change the face of a young actor the more made-up he looks, and hence the more you are impeding his performance.

What you need

You will often have to purchase very specific items of make-up for particular plays, but a good basic equipment for any drama club would include the following:

Leichner's theatrical make-up

This is sold in 'sticks' and 'liners'. These are of different colours and shades of colour, and some of them are known by numbers and some by the name of their colour. The difference between 'sticks' and 'liners' is that the sticks are not unlike cigars in appearance and are usually applied liberally and directly to the face or whatever other part of the body you are making-up, while liners are rather like small thin pencils and are usually applied very sparingly and, as their name implies, to draw lines with rather than to colour whole areas. In actual practice, not many actors use liners directly on the area they are making-up because you cannot achieve the fine precision even with a liner that you may need, and also because you may wish to mix colours and then to apply the mixture. Hence some actors use the palm of their left hand as a kind of palette in which they mix the various colours until they get the colour they need, and then apply it with a paint brush.

You will need a generous supply of the following *sticks*:

Number	3½	pale pink
Number	4½	brownish pink
Number	5	pale yellow
Number	8	dark tan
Number	9	brick red
Number	15	orange brown

Carmine I and Carmine II
and the following *liners*:

Lake
Medium Brown
Dark Brown
Black

Theatrical make-up and all the various by-products can be purchased in most major chemists, or if needs be from many costume hirers.

Removing cream

There are various makes. Removing cream is used in large quantities, not only for the obvious purpose of removing make-up after a performance, but also to prepare the skin before the make-up is applied.

White powder

White baby powder is the best. It is dusted on very liberally to stop the make-up from running during the performance. Many firms manufacture what is called 'blending powder', though exactly how a powder manages to 'blend' the make-up is anybody's guess.

Paper tissues

A liberal quantity is needed for wiping off the make-up and removing cream after the performance.

Mirrors

If you are not lucky enough to have proper dressing-room facilities in your school where sizeable mirrors are provided underneath strong lights, then you may have to provide good-sized shaving mirrors for each actor.

Powder puffs

These are used for dusting the powder on to the face. Some actors also use them for dusting the powder off with, but this can easily smudge the make-up.

Powder brushes

These are used to dust down the powder after it has been applied to the face. No sign of powder should be left showing.

Paint brushes

Use very good quality brushes, which are thin and firm. They are used for applying either single or mixed colours where a very firm clear line is needed. The best kind of brush is that which can be unscrewed from its stem and placed inside it to protect the brush from damage.

Liquid make-up

You may not ever have to use this. It is used to cover whole areas of the body with specific colours, and can be bought in almost any colour you may require.

Eye shadow

Should only be used for the ladies of the company. You will need blue, grey and green eye shadow.

Mascara

Ask the ladies to purchase whatever they need— usually black.

Spirit gum and surgical spirit

You will need these only if you are going to use false beards, moustaches or sideboards.

Crêpe hair

Used for making false hair, beards, moustaches and sideboards.

It is also a good idea for each individual actor to collect his own set of make-up around him, but even where this is not possible every actor ought to come to dress rehearsals and performances with the following:

    paper tissues

    soap and towel

    hand-mirror

    paint brush

    powder puff

Who should apply the make-up?

The common practice in school productions is to recruit a teacher, who appears to know something about make-up, to apply it to the actors' faces, or to recruit some outsider for the purpose. The actor then looks in the mirror at the end of this operation and sees what has been done to him. This of course completely ruins the whole purpose of school productions which is that the actors should learn how to do things themselves. This is not only more educational but also more enjoyable. And putting on one's own make-up is a wonderful way of relaxing before a performance and helps an actor to master his nerves and to begin to enjoy himself. Furthermore the purpose of make-up is that it should complement an actor's performance, and this can only be the case if the actor applies it himself. The actor must of course know what he is doing before he can apply his own make-up, and the best way to do this is to have a couple of practice sessions at which someone who does know how to do it demonstrates on a couple of the actors while all the others watch and then practise doing it for themselves. When they are making-up for the actual performances they will need one person to be around to tell them whether they have put on too little or too much, and this can be done by the assistant producer.

What is the purpose of stage make-up?

Stage make-up is only necessary in school plays in order to keep the actors' faces clearly visible to the audience. This is necessary partly because of the distance of the actor from his audience, and also because of the powerful lighting which is directed at the actor, and which tends to flatten the face and make it appear vaguely ghost-like. In a small hall one would tend to use less make-up than in a large one.

It is worth noticing that in some professional productions nowadays the actors use no make-up at all. This is usually because they are working in intimate theatres and are playing roles in which their own appearance is right for the character. This merely serves to emphasise that make-up is not essential on stage.

Before you make-up

(i) Do not attempt to make-up with all your costume on. Do not wear anything on the top part of the body which you are going to wear on stage. Remember that your neck has to be made up just as much as your face, and so the neck must be left bare while you are making up.

(ii) Massage a very small quantity of removing cream into all the parts of the skin where you are going to apply make-up. If you have a naturally oily skin this will not be necessary, otherwise it is advisable as a means of avoiding the skin-irritations which can be caused by the application of make-up. Once you have massaged the cream into the skin, remove all traces of it with tissue paper.

(iii) Make sure that you have plenty of light and a good mirror, so that you can see clearly what you are doing. Do not make up in a shady corner beneath the stage.

After you make-up

(i) Always powder the face liberally with white powder. This will stop the grease-paint from running when you are on stage. Then brush away the powder with a soft powder brush and make sure that no trace of the powder is showing.

(ii) Always wash your hands after you have finished making up, and then make up the back of the hands if necessary. If you have a bronze face the backs of the hands also should be quite dark. In that case, remember to powder the hands afterwards just as you did the face.

Removing make-up

Massage all the made-up areas of the face and body with removing cream and then wipe all the cream and the make-up off with paper tissues. Then wash in hot water and soap.

Straight make-up for young men

The base
Make lines all over the face and neck with the number 5 stick (pale yellow) and then with the number 8 stick (dark suntan) until your face looks like some primeval warrior's about to annihilate a neighbouring tribe. Then with the

tips of your fingers massage the colours into your face until the colouring is smooth and even. If you are fair-haired then use number 15 (orange brown) instead of number 8. Keep on adding 5 or 8 (or 15) until you get the right balance and your face looks healthily but not unnaturally sun-tanned. Under stage lighting you will then look fit and healthy.

When you are applying this base to your skin, make sure that you cover the entire face, including the forehead, temples and ears, and also including the backs of the ears and just below the ears. Do not go on stage with white ears and brown face. Also be sure to apply the same degree of make-up to the neck. Try not to get the grease-paint into the hair, but be sure not to leave a thin white line at the top of your forehead.

The cheeks

Using the stick of 9 (brick red) make a short line on each cheek bone and then massage this into the rest of the face. Make quite sure that you do not leave the impression of having rouged the cheeks. In particular make sure that the initial line is on the bone and not on the cheek itself. The effect should be to suggest more robustness around the cheek and cheek bones and to take away from the flatness of applying the same base to the entire face.

The eyes

There are many devices offered in books on make-up which are rather complex and are designed to make the eyes of middle-aged actors sparkle as if they were young. School actors do not need to bother with such nonsense. Hence they do not need eye-shadow, nor do they need little blobs of red at the corners of their eyes. Nor do they need to paint their eye-lids. All you need to do is:

take a brown liner (dark brown if your own colouring is dark, medium brown otherwise) and rub a small quantity into the palm of your left hand. With the fingers of the other hand rub the grease-paint into a larger circle so that the natural grease of the hand lubricates the paint and makes it moist. Now put the brush into the grease-paint so that you get a good quantity on to the brush, and paint a firm, thin line below the edge of the lower lid. See illustration *31*. Notice from the illustration that the line does not begin at the inside corner of the eye. It begins at roughly the middle of the lid and extends almost but not quite so far as the outer corner. It is painted firmly but thinly on the line formed by the roots of the lower lashes. If you are appearing in a rather large hall or theatre, or if you simply find that your eyes need additional prominence, then you can do the same thing to the upper lid, as

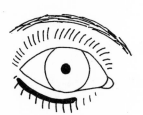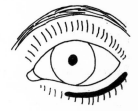

31   Basic eye make-up

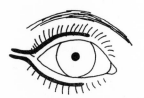

32   More distinctive eye make-up

in illustration *32*. Now clean your brush and the palm of the left hand with tissues, and do the same as you did with the brown liner only this time using the number 5 stick, putting a small quantity into the palm of the hand and then rubbing it in. Get a small quantity of this on to your brush and apply a firm thin line of pale yellow in between your two parallel lines of brown. This has the effect of enlarging and defining the eyes.

The eye-brows

The eye-brows usually need no make-up at all, but if you are concerned that your eye-brows are really too thin or too fair to stand out at all on a stage, then you can take your paint brush, get some medium brown on it in the way outlined for the eyes, and then very lightly brush the eye-brow following the actual line of the brow itself. Do not attempt to line the eye-brow so as to make a false one.

The lips

Make-up enthusiasts will urge you to do all manner of strange things to your lips. Don't. Leave them as they are after you have applied the base to your entire face. If you are then told that your lips are not prominent enough, or if you are appearing in a large theatre, you can perhaps go over the top lip lightly with the number 9 stick, and then rub the lips together so that you get the colouring on to both lips equally. Above all, never put carmine on to the lips, unless of course you are playing an extravagant fop in, say, Restoration Comedy, in which case you should make up your face much as a woman would do if she were appearing in the same play (i.e. with a very pale face, and highly defined lips and mouth, and with slightly rouged cheeks and a couple of black beauty spots).

The nose

The nose does not need any special make-up apart from the normal base. If you feel that the nose has become unduly flat under the make-up then you can lightly run the stick of 5 down the front of the nose from the bridge to the tip and then gently massage it in. This has the effect of highlighting the nose. You can, also, if you choose, put a touch of 5 on the side of each nostril and again massage in.

Straight make-up for young women

Base Sticks of number 5, 15 and $3\frac{1}{2}$. Mix freely and experiment till you get the right colour.
Cheeks Carmine II.
Eye-shadow Blue, grey or green according to the colour of the eyes. Use gold or silver if you need an exotic effect.
Eye-lines Black (on much the same principle as for men except that women can be much more obviously made-up). Also black for lining the eye-brows. Fair-haired women would use dark brown.
Eye-lashes Mascara.
Lips Carmine I or II.

Character make-up

The character should come from the actor's performance and not from his make-up. If you are playing a mean miserly character then there is no need to paint meanness and miserliness on to your face, even if such a thing is possible. If you are an actor your face will change in various subtle ways with each character you play, but do not waste time trying to paint the character on to yourself.

Adding age

If you are playing a much older character then all you need to do as regards make-up is to modify your base. Instead of the robust base that you use for young characters, use a base of 5 (pale yellow) mixed with 15 (orange brown) and $4\frac{1}{2}$ (brownish pink). This gives the impression of late middle age. Obviously with a much older character you will make the base even paler by using more of number 5. For the very old you may want to pale the lips down by brushing on thin lines of 5 vertically down the lips, and alternating with thin lines of lake. To add further age to the eyes, shade in the sockets of the eyes with brown, or lake and brown, applying it with a paint brush first, and then rubbing in with the finger tips. You can also highlight the cheekbone with number 5 and then shade the cheeks with a mixture of lake and brown. This makes the bones of the cheeks more prominent and makes the cheeks themselves appear to sink inwards. The highlighting and the shading must of course be massaged and blended into the rest of the face. Shade in the temples in the same way.

Before attempting to make up your face to look old, you should study paintings of old people. Notice that every effect is achieved by the use of contrast between light and shade. So if, for example, you shade heavily under the eyes to suggest age and tiredness, this has to be made effective by very light colouring (number 5) underneath the shading. This principle of shading and highlighting is the basis of all stage make-up.

The best way to begin is to collect photographs of old people, put these up in front of you, and start to experiment with your make-up.

Always remember that the way you move is far more important than your make-up, especially when it comes to playing older people. An audience will accept a young actress as a middle-aged mother if she moves with the right kind of weight and balance. The same principle applies to any age that you may be playing. The audience will not complain that you were not made up to look old, provided you capture the right kind of movement. One might extend the point a stage further, and say that it is the acting that counts, not the paint on your face.

Adding whiteness to the hair

The simplest way is to powder it with white hair powder or talcum powder, and to keep on combing the hair and re-powdering until you get the right intensity. If you want the hair to look a distinguished silver rather than generally grey you should buy from a chemist one of the various silver powders that women use on their hair. These are usually applied with a small brush. Be very moderate in the use of these, as they can be harmful to the hair if used too heavily. These silver powders are specially useful if you want to streak the hair with silver lines rather than cover it all over. To get a more completely white effect you should buy zinc oxide powder from a chemist and mix it with water to form a paste and then brush it into your hair.

Wigs

Do not use wigs unless absolutely necessary. To look really good on stage wigs need to fit an actor perfectly, and this is difficult to achieve, especially as few hirers of wigs will arrange fittings for you. Also the cheaper kind of wig shows a large fringe of thin material across the top of the forehead with which the wig grips the head, and the effect of the fringe is to make the actor look faintly ridiculous. The better wigs have a piece of hair-lace which does the same job of keeping the wig in place, but the lace is stuck on to the forehead and is virtually invisible. Unfortunately when you hire wigs you never know in advance which kind of wig you are going to get and also never know whether it will fit well.

Beards, sideboards and moustaches

Actors usually make these from crêpe hair. This hair is sold by the yard and is plaited tightly with string which causes the hair to crinkle. To eliminate this you cut off the amount of hair you will need and hold it stretched over a steaming kettle until the crinkles disappear. The beard is made by cutting off small portions of the hair and then sticking them with spirit gum on to the chin, building the beard up in this way until it acquires a naturalistic thickness and width. Make sure that you do not let the line formed by the 'roots' of the beard across the chin become a straight line. Once the beard is on, you can trim it to whatever length you want. Surgical spirit is used to remove beards.

Sideboards and moustaches are made on the same principle. Usually moustaches are made with a slight margin down the middle, but this depends on the type of moustache. Remember with sideboards that they should be bushy and should not give the appearance of hanging.

As a general principle be very sparing in the use of crêpe hair. Also, before attempting to make up a beard, moustache or sideboard, collect photos of them and use them as models.

Bruises and black eyes

Bruises Paint the area of the bruise quite liberally with a mixture of lake and brown. Then highlight the edges of the bruise with the number 5 stick. If you want the bruise to look especially sore, then you should go over the surface of the bruise with a thin veneer of removing cream.
Black eyes Paint the lids and sockets and below the lids with a circle of lake and brown mixed. Then highlight the edge of the black eye with number 5. To emphasise, lightly grease the top of the bruise with removing cream.

XVI *The Performance*

The producer

During performances he should not be seen at all backstage. He should sit in the audience and make notes on any aspect where he can help the actors to improve their work at the next performance. These notes should be given to the company either after the performance or an hour or so before the next performance. The producer's notes should help the actors over any unexpected hurdles they may meet when having to cope with a live audience. They may find that having to walk through an actual door, as opposed to walking through a space at rehearsals, alters their timing quite fundamentally. Or the actors may tend to pause at the second performance in the vain hope of getting the same laughs that they got at the first performance, and then they may be quite at sea when it comes to the third performance. Or an actor may suddenly begin to drop his voice at various points of the play, and in a manner which he has not done at rehearsals. In cases such as this, the actor may be quite unaware of what he is doing. Also, the producer's notes may be necessary simply to maintain the morale of the company. Actors are sometimes bitterly disappointed and depressed after the first performance simply because it is usually rather less brilliantly successful than they had hoped. The producer's notes are then necessary just to convince them that nevertheless the performance went well, and that first performances never are the best.

The stage manager

The only remaining job of the stage manager which needs some mention is the management of the curtain calls. The usual practice is for the producer to rehearse with his cast the sort and number of curtain calls that he wants. In this way the cast and the stage management know exactly what they have to do, and the show is not spoiled by clumsiness and fumbling. Producers should have imaginative curtain calls wherever possible, rather than the traditional bobbing up and down of the players with the rise and fall of the curtain. Weave the curtain calls into the whole style of the play and the production.

The actors

Getting ready

The actors should arrive at least half an hour before the show is due to begin. Preferably they should be there an hour before, but this is up to the actor himself. Never hurry the process of getting made-up and getting your costume on, for the preparation is itself relaxing.

At performance

The actor's job at the performance is to repeat what he has done at rehearsal with just the added intensity and projection to allow for the presence of the audience.

Actors may need to be reminded that every actor is nervous before he goes on stage. Nerves are necessary, and it is doubtful if you could go on to a stage and give a performance without them. Nervousness prepares you for the enormous output of energy that you need to sustain a performance.

Backstage

The atmosphere in the dressing-rooms and backstage should be a peaceful one. Many actors become depressed if there is a lot of noise in the dressing-rooms. If some of the actors need to sing at the tops of their voices then they should by all means be allowed to do so, but they should be given a room where they can do this without disturbing those who want peace and quiet. It is often a splendid idea to give the whole cast a warming-up session on stage about half an hour before the performance, at which everybody sings, dances, and generally limbers up.

While actors are waiting to go on stage, whether in the wings or in the dressing-rooms, they should show the greatest respect for each other. Some actors are distracted if other people come up and start talking to them just as they are about to enter the stage. In particular, a practical joker should be removed from the cast at the first signs of his existence, and his part given to his understudy.

The stage manager should allow no one backstage either before or during a performance. Interval visitors can destroy an actor's morale without having any intention of doing so, and can easily destroy his concentration.

As a general policy, actors should not tell each other the names of people who are sitting out front at particular performances. This too can destroy the actor's concentration, and when he is on stage it is essential that his mind should be uncluttered by thoughts of anything other than what he actually has to do.

Audiences

The inexperienced actor is often thrown by the fact that the audience behaves in different ways at different performances. This can cause a complete production suddenly to sag and lose spirit. This happens especially with comedies, where the audience laughs uproariously one night, and only occasionally the next. The actor should be warned that this will happen. No two audiences are ever the same, and no matter how experienced or inexperienced a cast may be, the audience dictates to some extent the rhythm and speed of a performance. This does not mean that the actor should consciously alter his performance. The skill of the actor lies in maintaining his work at the same pitch from one performance to the next, but the audience's reaction inevitably has its effect. For instance in the playing of comedy the actors have to learn how to hold on to the line of action through the inevitable breaks caused by the laughter.

When the audience laughs

There are four possible mistakes which an actor may make when his audience starts to laugh:

(i) He may laugh too, either at himself or his fellow actors. This sounds ridiculous, but it nevertheless happens very frequently. Never laugh at yourself on stage, or at other actors. You will notice with professional comics that the best of them never laugh at their own jokes, and they could laugh much more legitimately than can an actor in a play. It destroys the subtle fabric of the audience's belief in what is happening.

(ii) He may begin to play up to the audience. This is often effective in a superficial way, but the audience quickly tires of it, and to a much greater extent than the actor on stage may ever realise. It also wrecks the whole balance of the production. This kind of lapse into megalomania should be avoided at all times, except of course in music hall or pantomime, where a skilful performer can turn it to great advantage. In an actual play the performer should get his satisfaction from maintaining his performance through the audience's laughter.

(iii) He may give the audience too long in which to laugh. This is far more deadly in its effect than is the opposite fault, giving the audience too little time in which to laugh. Providing you add to the power of your projection, so that you are clearly heard above the laughter, it is never a bad idea to give the audience too little time in which to laugh. As a general principle, never let the audience have as much time to laugh as they would seem to like to have. If you think the audience are going to carry on laughing for half a minute, then allow them about a third of that time, then project powerfully to cut through the laughter and carry on with the play. This technique cannot be mastered the first time you walk on the stage but it is worth aiming at even then. Sometimes the best advice to beginners is not to stop for laughs at all, but to act right through them, simply raising the volume of vocal projection a shade higher until the laughter subsides. If actors pause for the full length of a laugh they not only destroy the whole pace and rhythm of a play, they also kill the audience's laughter. If you pause long enough you discourage the audience from laughing again. This is why you must learn to ride through the audience's laughter. The effect is to leave the pace of the play intact and to leave the audience ready to laugh again. In particular, never stop for laughs in the first half of a play. Ride over all laughs that occur before (say) the last half hour of the play.

(iv) He may respond too obviously to the behaviour of the audience. This may take the form of over-acting because he thinks the audience is in love with him, or of losing confidence because he thinks the audience disapproves of him. The latter often happens when a good audience on the first night is followed by a bad audience on the second. Actors should be warned that audiences are not only different but do not always show their enjoyment audibly. Some audiences laugh very little but yet enjoy the play very much indeed. The actor must have the nerve and the confidence not to let his performance disintegrate when the audience does not send out audible signals of approval.

Emergencies
Some kind of emergency arises during almost every performance, whether amateur or professional. Unless it involves some kind of mortal injury it should not cause the show to collapse in ruins. The usual kind of emergency takes one of two forms: either the actor forgets his lines or forgets to come on stage at the right moment, or alternatively a prop is mislaid and the actor who has to go on stage to shoot the villain cannot find the gun. As regards the first instance, if an actor forgets his lines, the other actors on stage should help him out until he comes back to the right line. Some actors are remarkably adept at this, and can help the other actor out without departing in any way from the style of the author. Actors should be prepared for the possible forgetting of lines. Provided the actor has honestly learnt the part he is playing, then it should not be held against him that he forgets a line or two at a performance. Very often this can be caused by an unexpected reaction from the audience. Tell your actors to look upon this as an occupational hazard. Train them to cope with it. Give them various exercises at rehearsal; e.g. improvise a scene where an actor develops a nose-bleed just before he has to go on, and the rest of the cast have to maintain the scene for five minutes till the actor is ready to enter. Tell them that you expect them to sail through such emergencies and that this is part of the excitement of acting. Give them an improvisation in which a chair collapses just as someone is about to sit on it; let this happen to an irate Victorian father, or to a king who has just made a magnificent entrance. Encourage your actors to enjoy the opportunities for improvising which emergencies present.

Postscript

When the production is over, do not let the work of the drama club come to a standstill. Continue with regular sessions of improvisation, play-reading and discussion until you are ready to launch out on the next production. Wherever possible, organise outings to the live theatre, to the cinema, to ballet and to opera. Get your company interested in the many different styles of play-writing. Let their work in the drama club develop not only their self-confidence but also a generous attitude to the performing arts in general. Encourage them to be experimental in the entertainments which they patronise, so that as adults their interest in theatre will extend beyond the traditional limits of bedroom farce and the spectacular West End musical. Try not to mislead your actors into thinking that success in the school play means that they should be stars of the London and New York stage, even though you may occasionally feel strongly tempted to do this. Do not encourage every good actor to become professional, nor even to go to drama school.

The purpose of the school play is not to provide a breeding ground for the theatrical profession, but to provide every student, who wishes to take advantage of it, the chance to speak out in front of others, to develop his imagination, his poise and his assurance, and to be part of a large and complex project to which he can actively contribute and in which he can achieve an excellence which is perhaps denied him in the rest of his life and work at school. It does not matter if the pupil never again participates actively in the theatre, whether on an amateur or a professional basis. The important thing is that he has developed socially, personally and artistically from the project. That is its sole justification.

Further Suggestions for Plays

I Remember Mama	John van Druten
On Monday Next	Philip King
The Cure for Love	Walter Greenwood
The Trial of Mary Dugan	Bayard Veiller
The Miracle Worker	William Gibson
Inherit the Wind	Lawrence and Lee
Caine Mutiny Court-Martial	Herman Wouk
Tom Jones	Joan Macalpine (adapted from Fielding)
Life with Father	Lindsay and Crouse
Cyrano de Bergerac	Edmond Rostand
The Love of Four Colonels	Peter Ustinov
Romanoff and Juliet	Peter Ustinov
The Silver Tassie	Sean O'Casey
Becket	Jean Anouilh
Cavalcade	Noel Coward
Spring 1600	Emlyn Williams
The Admirable Crichton	J. M. Barrie
Adventure Story	Terence Rattigan
Hobson's Choice	Harold Brighouse
Blithe Spirit	Noel Coward
Hay Fever	Noel Coward
Dandy Dick	Arthur Pinero
Luther	John Osborne
Tobias and the Angel	James Bridie
A Man for All Seasons	Robert Bolt
Ross	Terence Rattigan

Billy Liar	Waterhouse and Hall
Penny for a Song	John Whiting
Gammer Gurton's Needle	Sixteenth century Farce (Anonymous)
Knight of the Burning Pestle	Beaumont and Fletcher
The Miser	Molière
Mozart	Sacha Guitry
Golden Boy	Clifford Odets
Liliom	Ferenc Molnar
Tovarich	Deval (adapted by Sherwood)
My Three Angels	Husson (adapted by Spewack)
Jacobowsky and the Colonel	Werfel (adapted by Behrman)
Hamp	John Wilson
The Hamlet of Stepney Green	Bernard Kops
Hostile Witness	Jack Roffey
Stephen D.	Hugh Leonard

Musical Plays

The Wizard of Oz	Elizabeth F. Chapman
The Fantasticks	Jones and Schmidt
Follow that Girl	Slade and Reynolds
On the Level	Millar and Grainer
Jorrocks	Cross and Heneker
Joey, Joey	Moody, Waterhouse and Hall
Let's Make an Opera	Benjamin Britten
The Duenna	Sheridan (Slade adaptation)
England, Our England (musical revue)	Hall, Waterhouse and Moore

Play Publishers

John Calder Limited
17 Sackville Street W1

Evans Plays
Montague House
Russell Square WC1

Faber and Faber Limited
24 Russell Square WC1

Samuel French Limited
26 Southampton Street WC2

Methuen and Co. Limited
11 New Fetter Lane EC4

J. Garnet Miller Limited
54 Victoria Street SW1

Penguin Books Limited
Harmondsworth Middlesex

Censorship of New Material

New scripts must be submitted to the Lord Chamberlain for his approval, together with a fee of 2 guineas. The address is: The Comptroller, The Lord Chamberlain's Office, St James's Palace, London, S.W.1. No public performance of any kind may be given in this country until the Lord Chamberlain's licence has been obtained.

Index